Owls and Artificers

Owls and Artificers

Oxford Lectures on Poetry

Roy Fuller

The Library Press
New York
1971

International Standard Book Number 0–912050–06–3
Library of Congress Catalog Card Number 70–158611

Printed in Great Britain

Contents

	Foreword	7
I	Philistines and Jacobins	9
II	'Woodbine Willie' Lives!	27
III	An Artifice of Versification	44
IV	Both Pie and Custard	69
V	The Filthy Aunt and the Anonymous Seabird	89
VI	How to Stuff Owls	108
	Index	133

Foreword

This book consists of the first six lectures I gave, during 1969 and 1970, as Professor of Poetry in the University of Oxford, to which Chair I was elected in November 1968. I am very glad to be able to acknowledge here my gratitude to the Board of the Woolwich Equitable Building Society for understandingly consenting to my being nominated: at that time I held a full-time appointment with the Society. I have added a little additional material as postscripts to some of the lectures, and made a few revisions, but I have not changed their form as addresses to an audience, which the sympathetic reader will, I hope, have often in mind.

R. B. F.

I

Philistines and Jacobins

It is just a hundred years since the publication of Matthew Arnold's *Culture and Anarchy*. The first chapter of that book was originally his farewell lecture as Professor of Poetry at Oxford. It bears the title — if one dare utter the words now, even in Oxford — 'Sweetness and Light'.

One hundred years sounds a reasonable enough period for Arnold's topics in that last lecture to have become superannuated. Certainly the terms he used will seem to us curiously simple. This is partly due to his extraordinarily clear and unifying mind. But mainly we have the sense that time is on his side, a sense I think he shared, despite the urgency of his tones. The two lustra during which he occupied this Chair — unlike most of us he was good for a second term — were very far from being socially stagnant or politically calm, but the notion of material progress and fairly general peace could be reasonably held on to by even a sceptical member of the English middle-class. In my own times the question of culture has been bedevilled by the threats to culture's very existence. There have been two widespread wars, extremely destructive of property and human beings. At the end of the 'twenties there was a breakdown in world trade and a throttling of productive forces that could well have led to the permanent degeneration of the material basis of life. And finally the period has given birth to ideas, infinitely more pernicious than those held by the social classes Arnold christened Barbarians and Philistines, which proposed to destroy culture and produced, as the means of doing so, elaborately organized armed bands, places of torture and a large bureaucracy. But if we take a step away from the confusion resulting from such events — if we try, however feebly, for the uncluttered Arnoldian perspectives — it must surely strike us that in our day to day, even year to year, concerns how vague our grasp is of the central concepts of culture, and of how right Arnold was to concern himself with those concepts, even at the risk of over-simplification and wrong prediction. Taking the same risk, I want to see how his century-old ideas stand up, and in particular to apply some of his useful and imaginative terminology to the conditions of today.

Lionel Trilling, as long ago as 1939, pointed out in his masterly book on Arnold that although the phrase 'sweetness and light' had fallen into disrepute and had come to mean 'a smirking, simpering flabbiness of attitude' it had its origin in Jonathan Swift. 'In *The Battle of the Books* the debate between the spider and the bee is an allegory of the struggle between the Moderns and the Ancients. The bee has the best of it because he fills his hive "with honey and wax; thus furnishing mankind with the two noblest of things, which are sweetness and light".' Culture, Arnold says, has its origin in the love of perfection and 'it moves by the force, not merely or primarily of the scientific passion for pure knowledge, but also of the moral and social passion for doing good'. 'The notion of perfection,' he goes on to say, 'as culture brings us to conceive it' is 'a perfection in which the characters of beauty and intelligence are both present, which unites' those 'two noblest of things, sweetness and light.'

In this first chapter of *Culture and Anarchy* Arnold is not just combating the Philistinism, the ignorance of culture, of the middle-classes. He is conscious that the high-tide of Victorian prosperity is enveloping — or is likely to envelop — other classes. His argument is that only culture can bring home to those classes that prosperity is not enough, that only culture can say to them: consider the middle-class, 'their way of life, their habits, their manners, the very tones of their voice; look at them attentively; observe the literature they read, the things which give them pleasure, the words which come forth out of their mouths, the thoughts which make the furniture of their minds; would any amount of wealth be worth having with the condition that one was to become just like these people by having it?' The intervening hundred years have shown the fallacy in what Arnold took for granted — the inevitability of increasing prosperity and its increasing spread. They have shown how hazardously poised the system of production and distribution is that will even guarantee to everyone mere freedom from hunger. And so, in a period like the present, when in England prosperity has once more spread its so-called benefits, those benefits are widely thought to be good in themselves. History seems only to have succeeded in entrenching more deeply the notion that Arnold attacked, the belief in prosperity as a good in itself, with the correlative prospect that, as he said, 'the whole world, the future as well as the present, would inevitably belong to the Philistines.' Nor, alas, is the confidence in affluence *simpliciter* confined to the middle-classes.

It is the revolt against mere material prosperity that constitutes a large part of today's revolt of the young, and which takes place in the minds and conduct of the young as individuals quite apart from their action as members of groups. Even the offspring of the intelligentsia revolt, by way of dropping out from education, rash erotic alliances, crumminess of appearance, and so forth, perhaps because they see their parents more and more obsessed by the gadgets of affluence and less and less convinced that anything can be done by way of principle and belief. What is disturbing is that youth's rebellion is not specifically against the spreading Philistinism that Arnold so clearly saw as a concomitant of the spread of affluence but indeed is often productive itself of Philistinism of another kind.

The extraordinary view has been put forward, perhaps most persuasively by T. R. Fyvel, that the coming into power of the Labour Party in 1945 resulted in a social revolution — that round about 1950 we were propelled into a new type of society. This society is no longer run by some privileged minority but by intellectuals in their roles as managers, technicians and purveyors of art. In the 'thirties, the argument runs, the efforts of English writers to step out of their class and reach a wider audience was premature: only recently has a society been achieved into which they could integrate. And so there is a widespread confidence that the intellectual can fulfil his role in our society by actually earning his living — an affluent living — as an intellectual. The intellectuals are bamboozled — or bamboozle themselves — into thinking, for example, that because there is a big audience for the Colour Supplement or the cultural TV programme they are completely realizing themselves as intellectuals by satisfying that audience. There could be no greater danger than in imagining that our society is yet so organized as to owe the intellectual a living.

Of course, nowadays many factors have combined to blur the distinctions between the categories of art that for want of better terms I will call highbrow, middlebrow and kitsch. But that these categories exist and will continue to exist in our society and are distinguishable I have not the slightest doubt. What is more, despite the confusion of the cultural scene — indeed, perhaps because of it — I believe it essential to go on distinguishing them. The middlebrow masquerades as the highbrow as it always has, though possibly more strangely than ever before. Thus prompted by the predigestive processes of television John Galsworthy re-emerges — not with his pretensions as a serious novelist discredited (though that job was done forty years ago) and not merely capturing middlebrow eyes and ears, but finding apologists among critics of nominally highbrow cast. However, that is a fairly harmless and maybe fleeting example. But where is the review and where the critics who will deal with the pretensions of the novelists of the 'sixties? Some such too highly estimated fictioneers are American and in this field America has often over-called its hand mainly because of the relative paucity of its cards. But others are British, often British females, though it is not mere chauvinism or chivalry that leads to them being so gently handled. Our noted critics — so learned and subtle — seem in-capable of fulfilling criticism's primary task, that of telling us whether the work of art under consideration is any good or not.

Scarcely, as they say, were those words dry when two long reviews of a new novel conveniently appeared. 'Why is the biographical detail handled with such farcical briskness?' asked reviewer A. 'Because,' he said, 'there is no time to be lost in getting everyone thrown into the great centrifuge of love; because there are to hand squads of significant detail, of easy, surprising, symbol-concealing dialogue . . . It leads us, if we can follow, down to the rite or formula which the book is half-hiding. Not that all is concealment; there is sometimes a suspicious candour. The power station and the cemetery are very large symbols of love and death . . . There are meditations, sometimes direct, sometimes oblique, on Last Things, on the necessary and the contingent, on time as we experience it in dying and in reading novels, on ritual as a means of reversing the flow of time. If, in the end, we are consoled, rather than made to think on these things, we are . . . either contingent persons, or we are dealing with only a minor work of art.' The critical question with which that pas-sage begins proves to be merely rhetorical because it is never answered in value-assessing terms; and the alternatives which the critic expresses in almost every sentence leave the reader almost as bemused as the critic himself. Reviewer B is also intent on giving herself a series of let-outs. 'The central theme of the novel,' she remarks, 'could baldly be said to be the unity of Love and Death — a grand description which could mean everything or nothing. What it primarily means in terms of the human action of the story is that sudden passionate love is analogous to the apprehension of death, in that it concentrates a man's mind wonderfully. It is also implied that the violence and intensity engendered by love are, in a world of imperfect harmony, at least as likely to destroy the loved object as to preserve it. The love which is death is perhaps one of those themes which has to be fully embodied in literature to be meaningful . . . The reader's attention is constantly deflected from the action, the physical world, loves and deaths, to the statements: God is death, All is One. The characters merge into each other, the dead and the living bound up indistinguishably in a spider's web of relationships, similarities of temperament, repeated situations, so that there appear finally to be one man and one woman, both — like the Indian deities, Shiva and Parvati, who are invoked throughout the book — waving innumerable arms in a dance of love and destruction.' What strikes one here is that the discussion, the explication, is quite remote from experience as we know it, though what is being discussed is intended to be a depiction of life. It would not have been difficult to find parallel passages in contemporary criticism of poetry where the critic was sufficiently elevated and similarly convinced of the sanctity of his subject.

As for kitsch, I suppose the expansion of its manufacture in our society was inevitable having regard to the greater leisure, affluence and sophistication of the mass audience. But kitsch has also been successful in capturing an audience that once would not have looked beyond middlebrow or, astonishingly enough, highbrow art. Not a great deal of surprise is excited when the music critic of *The Times* finds on a gramophone record of the latest kitsch the best songs since Schubert — a statement made with no doubt deliberate and possibly humorous hyperbole but implying nonetheless that Brahms, Duparc, Debussy, Strauss, Rachmaninov and Poulenc had been weighed in the balance and found wanting. A similar phenomenon may be seen in the James Bond and Liverpool poets cults — a self-destructive urge by highbrow and middlebrow critics to jump on the band-wagon perhaps through exhaustion of ideas or a sense that the organs they serve require their readers to be mollified or outraged. This is the elevation of kitsch, a chronic disability to take it for what it is. The disease is recurring but as short-lived as the bug that causes it. Far more dangerous is the substitution of kitsch. The music critic already mentioned has recently written: 'If the essence of Bach, Mozart and the Beatles has bitten into a person, that person today will ... listen delightedly to The Incredible String Band and Tyrannosaurus Rex, Bob Dylan, Jacques Loussier, Simon and Garfunkle, T-Bone Walker, Julian Bream, Ewan MacColl, and Stockhausen.' Again, for journalistic purposes, the list has deliberately outrageous intent. But the coupling of the Beatles with Bach and Mozart is surely meant to give the reassurance that after all the *St Matthew Passion* and *The Marriage of Figaro* are only made up of tunes and rhythms, while the appearance of Stockhausen's among the other artistically limited names has an appropriateness the author did not presumably intend.

The Philistinism of the middle-class of Arnold's time arose from their belief that wealth and material progress were sufficient to prove England's greatness and well-being. It was their ignoring culture he complained about. A similar Philistinism exists, of course, today, but one is tempted to say that our chief cultural evil is not lack of interest but lack of standards. Though our history has impoverished the private patron it has brought a far wider assumption by government, local government and parents that culture should be supported. The motives for such support may be prestige, earning of foreign currencies, competitive education, the need of the economy for more sophisticated employees — anything, in fact, but fondness for the end product — but the actual disbursement of public doles raises acutely the question of standards in the art encouraged by them. (I refrain from saying anything — on this occasion — about the abilities of the recipients of such doles and the effect of the doles upon them.) Who but the independent critic can supply such standards and from where can such critics come except the universities? Where, indeed, except in the universities is the possibility of the intellectual earning his living by being an intellectual at full stretch?

There is today a Philistinism that Arnold would have recognized, though its impertinence and its source would have staggered him. It is the notion, expressed not by the golf club, the hunt ball or the chamber of commerce, but by those in or near political power, that learning is like the contents of a drill manual that can be passed on to raw recruits by some corporal who has been on a short course. That the authority to impart knowledge can only be acquired by the attempt to extend knowledge one would have thought unchallengeable, but the lesson of the moment is that not even the fundamental principles of culture are safe from attack. As E. H. Gombrich has said, in a letter to *The Times* that merits less ephemeral publication, we do not know what causes the delicate plant of civilization to flourish but a blueprint for its destruction is to 'penalize intellectual curiosity by disparaging research, prevent the formation of public standards by discouraging publication, and empower the ignorant to determine the rating of the learned.' And perhaps I should add here that I think those dissatisfied with universities from below merely join hands with those who want to tinker from above when they demand freedom from their knowledge being assessed or freedom to pursue knowledge in some random and unhistorical mode. Such demands, such freedoms, I see merely as analogous to the insistence of many young creative artists to be relieved of the necessity of draughtsmanship or of ever arranging their verse in stanzas.

There is a famous passage in Arnold's last lecture from this Chair which occurs at the end of his anatomizing of the culture-less condition of the mere prosperity, the mere moral rigour, the mere freedom of speech of the industrial society of his day. 'Oxford,' he said, 'the Oxford of the past, has many faults; and she has heavily paid for them in defeat, in isolation, in want of hold upon the modern world. Yet we in Oxford, brought up amidst the beauty and sweetness of that beautiful place, have not failed to seize one truth: the truth that beauty and sweetness are essential characters of a complete human perfection. When I insist on this, I am all in the faith and tradition of Oxford. I say boldly that this our sentiment for beauty and sweetness, our senti-ment against hideousness and rawness, has been at the bottom of our attachment to so many beaten causes, of our opposition to so many triumphant movements. And the sentiment is true, and has never been wholly defeated, and has shown its power even in defeat. We have not won our political battles, we have not carried our main points, we have not stopped our adversaries' advance, we have not marched victoriously with the modern world; but we have told silently upon the mind of the country, we have prepared currents of feeling which sap our adversaries' position when it seems gained, we have kept up our own communications with the future.'

I do not regard those words, any more than the phrase 'sweetness and light', as sentimental or ineffectual or outmoded — though in ways Arnold did not foresee and at which he would have been appalled, our Oxford is not his nor our world an extension of his 'modern world'. Our material prosperity is far more precariously held than his. Our peace is not, as his was, divisible from wars elsewhere. Our philistinism, as I have said, contains a sleeping virus actually destructive of culture. We see more clearly than he did — though he was no fool in the matter — that culture and beauty, sweetness and light, are relative terms, meaningless except in historical contexts.

Again, I cannot help finding Arnold's expression of his democratic idea extremely moving. 'The sweetness and light of the few,' he said, 'must be imperfect until the raw and unkindled masses of humanity are touched with sweetness and light.' Insofar as he imagined that that touching could come about by a mere diffusion of culture his idea must nowadays be felt to be inadequate, for surely history proves that the horse of social change must be put before the cart of cultural enlightenment. All the same, standards can be achieved and maintained and learnt even in institutions that seem to be archaically organized, perhaps to serve a class purpose, to help preserve the *status quo* — even in Oxford. And those who go out from such institutions have no need to sacrifice those standards to the demands of the mass media or the requirements of earning a living — any more than a scientist need devote his career to biological warfare. To praise Miss X or Mrs Y in the weekly reviews; to pull one's punches in arts programmes on TV; to report wrong facts through slovenliness or prejudice — these are not absolutely inevitable consequences of an arts degree.

Of course, I realize that quite a few may hold the Maoist idea that culture, as we have inherited it, is so powerful that even after a profound social change it can corrupt the children of the revolution and of itself breed counter-revolution. And therefore that inherited culture is to be rejected root and branch. Perhaps it is being naïve and old-fashioned but I find such a notion anathema. For me it conjures up the ludicrous, pathetic but frightening picture of enraged Chinese on the steps of their embassy, in one hand a little book, in the other a wooden bludgeon. If a new social order cannot transform the cultural superstructure, something is sadly amiss with the social order. The whole socialist concept, it seems to me, is substantially justified not merely by its promise to make culture universally available but also by its capability of raising culture to only dreamed of heights.

Many of us will find Arnold's least sympathetic side in his rejection of what he called 'Jacobinism'. This he described in a later chapter of *Culture and Anarchy* as 'the violent indignation with the past, abstract systems of renovation applied wholesale, a new doctrine drawn up in black and white for elaborating down to the very smallest details a rational society for the future.' (And some of my audience might have found a passage in the first edition of *Culture and Anarchy* particularly offensive. 'As for rioting,' Arnold said there, 'the old Roman way of dealing with *that* is always the right one; flog the rank and file, and fling the ringleaders from the Tarpeian Rock.' But those words, quoted from his father, no doubt reasonably forged from the latter's experience as Headmaster of Rugby, were excised from later editions.)

Though Arnold was writing in the 1860s when the ideas of scientific socialism were already available, even in English, his Jacobins — Comte, Buckle, John Stuart Mill — seem to us now bogeymen who would scarcely alarm a reader of the *Daily Telegraph*. It is the great deficiency of *Culture and Anarchy* that at this point it burkes the issue of a revolutionary culture raised by the growth and organization and ideology of the working-class movement. And as the century wore on, the notion became almost a commonplace that the true heirs of culture were precisely those who quarrelled with the inadequacies of past societies and who had a blueprint for the future.

Arnold's view, that for Jacobinism culture 'is an impertinence and an offence' has in fact more relevance for these times than for his. For don't we see often manifested in present-day unrest, particularly when the revolt of youth occurs in isolation from that of the industrial working-class, not the notion that culture is to be rescued from those who are no longer fitted to be its guardians, that culture's scope and penetration is to be extended beyond its narrow confines, but rather an impatience with culture, even a despisal of it? The rejection of a set of disciplines felt to be merely repressive or unuseful is not proposed to be followed by the adoption of disciplines more apt but by the mere absence of discipline. It is, as I have said, as though a painter were to abandon not merely an academic school but also the necessity for draughtsmanship, or a poet to embrace free verse without ever having written a sonnet. This modern Jacobinism has nothing in common with the revolutionary ideals of the working-class — the concept of taking culture over and putting it to better use, just as the sophisticated organization of the factory is to be taken over, not destroyed.

What are revolutions for if not to increase the amount of sweetness and light? It is perhaps the present concentration on the trappings rather than the purpose of rebellion that has led to the rebels being characterized by some as not left-wing but unconsciously right-wing. Certainly we tend to forget, with the twilight of fascism most vividly in our memory, how that movement originated in extreme breakaways from the mass political parties of the left and how many of its leaders were failed artists. Goebbels, Hess, Baldur von Shirach, and even Ribbentrop had literary ambitions. According to the British Ambassador to Germany (and in this matter he was probably more reliable than in his assessment of other German affairs)

Hitler was saying, as late as 1939: 'All my life I have wanted to be a great painter in oils ... As soon as I have carried out my programme for Germany, I shall take up my painting. I feel that I have it in my soul to become one of the great artists of the age and that future historians will remember me not for what I have done for Germany, but for my art.'

The combination of ineffectual Bohemianism, artistic arrogance and political violence promises, to my mind, not social revolution but reaction. Such things are hallmarks not of the industrial working-class but of the petty bourgeoisie and the lumpen-proletariat. And here I would like to read from the pamphlet written by Lenin almost exactly fifty years ago called '*Left Wing Communism*': *an Infantile Disorder*. This remarkable passage has been a favourite of mine for — I can't say fifty years but certainly more than half that time. It is all the more remarkable in that it appeared before fascism had established itself as a mass political movement.

'It is not sufficiently known abroad that Bolshevism grew up, formed, and hardened itself in long years of struggle against *petty-bourgeois revolutionism*, which resembles, or borrows something from, anarchism. It differs in one respect or another, in all essentials, from the conditions and requirements of a consistent proletarian class-struggle. For Marxians it is well established theoretically — and the experience of all European revolutions and revolutionary movements fully confirms — that the small owner (the social type which in many European countries is very numerous and widespread), who, under capitalism, is constantly oppressed and suffering, and whose conditions of life often take a sharp and rapid turn for the worse, moves easily when faced with ruin to extreme revolutionism, but is incapable of displaying consistency, organisation, discipline and firmness. The petty-bourgeois, "gone mad" from the horrors of capitalism, is a social phenomenon which, like anarchism, is characteristic of all capitalist countries. The weakness of such revolutionism, its futility, its liability swiftly to transform itself into obedience, apathy, fantasy and even into a "mad" infatuation with some bourgeois "fashionable" tendency — all this is a matter of common knowledge. But a mere recognition in the abstract, a theoretical recognition of these truths, does not at all free revolutionary parties from old mistakes, which always appear unexpectedly in a somewhat new form, in new trappings, in more or less original surroundings.'

Is the whole of the West in a Weimar period? Is the dissatisfaction with government, with the very savour of day to day life, and the growing inability of government to govern, its insane multiplication of bureaucratic remedies and processes, going to lead to authoritarian régimes dedicated nakedly to national self-sufficiency and aggrandisement? These are questions that have even seeped down to the leaders and correspondence columns of newspapers, though there they may be overlaid by puerile or fleeting bees in the bonnet like coalition administrations and the rudeness of railway-car attendants.

Certainly anyone who lived through the 'twenties and 'thirties must feel unease, even dread, to see how many features of pre-fascist Germany are reappearing in Europe and America — features some of which are actually taken to be progressive or liberatory. The currency and inflationary parallels are obvious. But the exploitation of pornography in entertainment not only by the entrepreneurs of kitsch but also by nominally serious publishers, producers, writers and artists in the literary, dramatic and graphic fields is just as significant. And I leave to D. H. Lawrence to point the repetition of another phenomenon. Writing from Germany in 1924, he said: 'These queer gangs of *Young Socialists*, youths and girls, with their non-materialistic professions, their half-mystic assertions, they strike one as strange. Something primitive, like loose roving gangs of broken scattered tribes, so they affect one.' Needless to speculate how many such 'Young Socialists' became in a few years National Socialists. What if quantities of the young revolutionaries of Europe and America today proved to be the petty bourgeoisie 'gone mad' from the horrors of capitalism?

A central point of Arnold's last Oxford lecture — and he

certainly did not drag in this idea because he felt his remarks had strayed too far from the nominal scope of his Chair — is the equating of culture with poetry. In 'making sweetness and light to be characters of perfection,' he said, 'culture is of like spirit with poetry, follows one law with poetry.' And he added that the dominant idea of poetry was 'the idea of beauty and of a human nature perfect on all sides.' I am not sure that even in their context these remarks are entirely intelligible: certainly they need to be studied in the light of Arnold's conception of poetry which is spread over many years and many documents. But I think we must agree that of all the arts poetry must set within itself a standard of truth that transcends — I won't say the historical context of the poet: that would be impossible — but the frailty of the poet and the character of his subject. In the disgust of a Swift or the malice of a Pope, the accidie of an Eliot or the pride of a Yeats, there is being propounded a notion of beauty and of human perfection. This is not only — indeed, one is tempted to say this is least — shown in the poet's ideas, which are in fact the most likely to be at the mercy of history. Nor is it exclusively evidenced by his trouvailles of language and imagery — those 'touchstones' to which Arnold elsewhere attached such great importance. It is rather in the absence of pretence, of duplicity, of fudging, which poetry demands from its practitioners — disobedience to which requirement will sooner or later be discovered in the tell-tale stuff of the poem, the language common to the poet's countrymen.

Today, more than ever before, there is agreement with Arnold that culture must have a broad basis, that we 'must have sweetness and light for as many as possible'. Only, I would add, as Arnold added: 'it must be *real* sweetness and *real* light'. The poets of the so-called 'modern movement' have often been themselves to blame for poetry's giving in to its status as a minority art. The *Cantos* of Ezra Pound, for all their triumphs of versification and scattered felicities, are finally, as their author himself has admitted, a failure. They are a failure, one suggests, because they rely, in a falsely primitive way, in the magical power of words, of names;

because they rely on incoherence of narration to give significance to the story they tell. But this does not mean that poetry has a duty to become simple and straightforward. 'Plenty of people', as Arnold said, 'will try to give the masses . . . an intellectual food prepared and adapted in the way they think proper for the actual condition of the masses.' Poets today may safely leave naïvity, sentimentalism, nursery rhymes and metres, cosily naughty ideas and words, to the purveyors of kitsch, who can be depended upon to turn out the stuff in quantities quite sufficient to satisfy the profitable market for it. Poetry's success or excellence cannot yet be assessed by the magnitude of the audience that may turn up to hear it spouted or buy it on record or in paper-back.

Nor will it be so assessable after some social revolution has altered its function and the poet's status. The ludicrous and tragic history of Soviet poetry is evidence of that. It is no doubt true — and I once again quote Arnold — that 'he who is morbid is no adequate interpreter of his age'. But this does not mean, as official Marxist critics have often thought, that when poetry deals with human weakness or when it freshens its vision through experiments with new forms, it is being most typically bourgeois. Poetry will always have to deal with death, with human love, with the curiosities of the body, and with the anomalous and not altogether unmysterious place of organic life in a universe largely of quite different stuff — indeed, with the preposterousness of the universe itself. In this, it seems to me, it is no different from science, and who asks science to distort its findings or refrain from certain investigations except those with a political reason for suppressing the truth?

I must say I hesitated before deciding to end with what were Arnold's very last words in Oxford. The circumstances which led to one's being here at all were so different from the distinction that fitted Arnold for this office. And they were circumstances whose attendant vulgarities would have appalled him — though confirming his diagnosis of culture's ills — and perhaps would have caused him bitterly to regret his engineering the changing of the requirement that these lectures should be given in Latin.

Besides, Arnold's eloquence and high-mindedness might sound excessively odd after the crude words one had to offer oneself. But the centennial coincidence and my long respect for Arnold as critic and poet swung the balance in favour of inclusion. And possibly some will be unfamiliar with Arnold's peroration which more forcibly than anything I have said myself conveys the ideas I have been speaking around.

Culture, Arnold said, 'does not try to teach down to the level of inferior classes; it does not try to win them for this or that sect of its own, with ready-made judgments and watchwords. It seeks to do away with classes; to make the best that has been thought and known in the world current everywhere; to make all men live in an atmosphere of sweetness and light, where they may use ideas, as it uses them itself, freely — nourished, and not bound by them.

'This is the *social* idea; and the men of culture are the true apostles of equality. The great men of culture are those who have had a passion for diffusing, for making prevail, for carrying from one end of society to the other, the best knowledge, the best ideas of their time; who have laboured to divest knowledge of all that was harsh, uncouth, difficult, abstract, professional, exclusive; to humanise it, to make it efficient outside the clique of the cultivated and learned, yet still remaining the *best* knowledge and thought of the time, and a true source, therefore, of sweetness and light. Such a man was Abelard in the Middle Ages, in spite of all his imperfections; and thence the boundless emotion and enthusiasm which Abelard excited. Such were Lessing and Herder in Germany, at the end of the last century; and their services to Germany were in this way inestimably precious. Generations will pass, and literary monuments will accumulate, and works far more perfect than the works of Lessing and Herder will be produced in Germany; and yet the names of these two men will fill a German with reverence and enthusiasm such as the names of the most gifted masters will hardly awaken. And why? Because they *humanised* knowledge; because they broadened the basis of life and intelligence; because they worked powerfully to diffuse sweetness and light, to make reason and the will of God prevail.'

Most of us, I suppose, would want to substitute some other words for Arnold's phrase about making 'the will of God prevail'. No doubt here is the nub of our troubles. The founders of scientific socialism, with their detestation of tyranny, their passion for research, their guarded but sincere admiration for the giants of bourgeois culture — for Shakespeare, for Balzac — had no doubt that the ideals of the working-class completely filled the moral void left when the myth of religion became outworn. How incredulous they would have been if they had been told that in the second half of the twentieth century, socialists who had achieved political power could be more dangerously Philistine than the utilitarian capitalists of their own epoch; and that socialists seeking power could often seem to glorify the violence in society that socialism is committed to abolish. Most of all, perhaps, they would have been astonished that a wider diffusion of literature could be contemplated which was unaccompanied by increased technical mastery, increased realism, an increased absorption of the lessons and traditions of the past.

Of course, not even Arnold imagined that the will of God would prevail in some miraculous manner. He ended his lecture with the words of another Christian of like mind, St Augustine. 'Let us not leave Thee' — and the word had a capital letter — 'Let us not leave Thee alone to make in the secret of thy knowledge, as thou didst before the creation of the firmament, the division of light from darkness; let the children of thy spirit, placed in their firmament, make their light shine upon the earth, mark the division of night and day, and announce the revolution of the times; for the old order is passed, and the new arises; the night is spent, the day is come forth; and thou shalt crown the year with thy blessing, when thou shalt send forth labourers into thy harvest sown by other hands than theirs; when thou shalt send forth new labourers to new seed-times, whereof the harvest shall be not yet.'

POSTSCRIPT

The comment (page 22) on the failure of the *Cantos* drew a sharp question from G. Singh, who had written to Pound about it and received in reply a telegram which said (*inter alia*): 'STATEMENT RE CANTOS NOT MINE'. The reference I had in mind was a conversation Daniel Cory had with Pound in October 1966, as reported by Mr Cory in an article in *Encounter* (May, 1968). Eric Homberger answered Mr Singh by producing this reference, and also further reports of Pound's self-critical attitude to the poem. On this, Michael Reck made the comment that a poet's own view of his work was irrelevant to its value. (The correspondence is to be found in the *Times Literary Supplement* for March 6, 13, 27, and April 3, 1969.) With this last point I am very sympathetic, but Pound's doubts, however less straightforward than the brief remark in the lecture might have made them appear, do seem to fit the way the *Cantos* were composed, and the regrets felt by many readers of them.

Perhaps, too, since journalistic wonders are so quickly forgotten, a word is due about the reference (page 23) to the 'circumstances' of the 1968 election of the Professor of Poetry (the statutes requiring the vacancy to be filled through the personal votes of the Masters of Arts of the University). In the end many candidates were nominated, of varying degrees of suitability, and much popular ink was spilt about the personalities and manœuvrings involved, or said to be.

II

'Woodbine Willie' Lives!

I start by reading a stanza from a short poem:

One solace there is for me, sweet but faint,
As it floats on the wind of the years,
A whisper that spring is the last true thing
And that triumph is born of tears.

I haven't the slightest doubt that for many the lines will be familiar — they come, in fact, from Poem IV in the group of poems which I. A. Richards, during the 'twenties, circulated among his students at Cambridge. The various authorship of the poems was not revealed and the comments of the students — who also remained anonymous — was invited. Those comments formed the basis, of course, of Richards's celebrated book, *Practical Criticism*.

Forty years on from the publication of *Practical Criticism* we aren't likely to say of the poem from which I've quoted, as one of Richards's students said, referring particularly to the stanza I've read, that 'This is a fine poem written with deep, emotional feeling and a choice of words that is only possible for the genuine poet. The melancholy power of the whole is transformed into something greater by the inspiring and courageous thought of the last verse.' Or, rather, let me put it more cautiously: if we knew that this was a contemporary poem we wouldn't now be fooled by its content. My notion is, in fact, that the give-away of the poem's value is not so much its sentiments as its form. Today, the poem's internal rhymes and regular anapaests are enough to arouse suspicion of it and, unlike Richards's students, few or none would be greatly surprised to learn that the piece comes from a book called *More Rough Rhymes of a Padre* by the Reverend G. A. Studdert Kennedy, 'Woodbine Willie' of the First World War. I would like to try to judge whether forty years of Richards and Richards's followers have had any revolutionary effect on the reader's power to evaluate a poem, particularly by looking at the question of sentimentality. And, examining the other side of the medal, I would like to try to judge whether a poem may fool us by dressing itself fashionably, by appearing in an OK form. (And also I would like to say here that though it is my thesis that Woodbine Willie lives in some metaphysical sense, it must give us great pleasure that Dr Richards, beyond question one of the great men of my time, is alive in every sense.)

Sentimentality is merely one of ten 'difficulties of criticism' that Richards lists in the introductory chapter to *Practical Criticism*. These difficulties were here being simply 'roughly sketched', as Richards thought, but I have always felt that the question of sentimentality was a key one in the evaluating of poetry and that Richards might have said as much. In the analytical part of the book he devotes a chapter to sentimentality and what he regards as its twin danger, inhibition, but I think his discussion is altogether too canny and refined. It is true that among the intellectuals of the late 'twenties there was a greater horror of sentimentality than there is among intellectuals today, and the beginning of Richards's chapter is evidence of a backlash against the use of the term. He starts by warning of its indiscriminate employment as a mere vague term of abuse and though I suppose one ought still to pay attention to such a point I feel that the time has come round again when one needn't be too nice about this.

Certain of the intellectuals of the 'twenties, reacting against the general intellectual atmosphere, were at pains to show that the heart or the guts or the gonads were as important, or more so, than the head — hence the rather excessive sympathy in *Practical Criticism* with D. H. Lawrence's poem 'Piano' and Richards's initial severity about sentimentality as 'one of the most overworked words in the whole vocabulary of literary criticism'. I want to summarize briefly Richards's views of sentimentality and hope not to lose sight of them entirely, though I don't propose to apply them to any practical examples.

Richards distinguishes three senses of the word 'sentimental'.

First, he says, 'A person may be said to be sentimental when his emotions are too easily stirred, too light on the trigger.' This is the *quantitative* sense of sentimental — when the response is 'too great for the occasion'.

Secondly, Richards says that 'sentimental' may be used as an equivalent to 'crude'.

And, finally, 'A response is sentimental when, either through the over-persistence of tendencies or through the interaction of sentiments, it is inappropriate to the situation that calls it forth.' This *inappropriate* sense of sentimental is illustrated by Richards with some curiously trivial examples — for instance, a schoolmaster who in later life is discovered to be an unimportant and negligible person yet still retains his power to overawe.

Indeed, I think we must feel very strongly that something vital is missing from the whole analysis. The question in poetry of the right amount of feeling, of the refinement of feeling and of the appropriateness of feeling is obviously of fundamental importance, but we don't get the sense that here Richards is grappling with fundamentals at all. Undoubtedly, before the chapter ends he has said a few interesting things. For instance, when we apply the term sentimental to a poem we may mean either of two notions or we may mean both. We may mean that the author of the poem was sentimental or we may mean that we ourselves should be sentimental if we allowed ourselves to be moved by the poem. Sometimes both assertions can be true but Richards adds that often we are only entitled to make the assertion of sentimentality about ourselves, the readers. Here again is evidence of what I feel to be Richards's over-scrupulousness — however necessary in the context of Cambridge and the 'twenties — in not disallowing a poetry of overt emotion. It is true that in the immediately ensuing discussion of Woodbine Willie's poem Richards says that a poet need not be frightened away from topics that arouse sentimental feeling if he can give enough 'nearness, concreteness and co-herence' to such topics to support and control the response that ensues, but Richards adds in a footnote that he is not recommending nearness, concreteness and coherence as specifics for the avoidance of sentimentality.

Richards's *Practical Criticism* was published in 1929, the year of the outbreak of the world economic crisis. The effect of that event on English literature could hardly be better illustrated than by seeing how Richards's ideas about sentimentality fared in the context of the Marxist criticism of the ensuing period. I've said elsewhere how important Richards was to the establishment of the Auden school of poets or, more precisely, to the dominance of the poets, centred round Auden, who looked initially to Geoffrey Grigson's magazine *New Verse* for publication and critical support. Grigson himself, with his great interest in botany and the visual arts, would certainly have regarded the nearness, con-creteness and coherence in poetry as pretty effective warranties of its non-sentimentality. But in its early days at any rate and sustained by the first flowering of Auden's talent and influence, *New Verse* was hardly concerned with any deficiencies in Richards's critical methods.

It is in a book called *Crisis and Criticism* by Alick West, pub-lished in 1937, that the 'thirties critical case is, I believe, most clearly and subtly put — though, I am bound to add, the case is by no means convincingly clinched, nor did it even seem so at the time of publication. However, as is common with Marxist works, its polemic is more effective than its positive conclusions, and its discussion of Richards is still most suggestive. I'm sustained in my belief in the importance of the subject of sentimentality by

Alick West taking up that very question as the starting point of his chapter on Richards. West finds Richards's analysis unsatisfactory though he recognizes that the problem is complex and that any approach can only be tentative. His own is to treat the question as a social question and to start with a text from *The Communist Manifesto*. But it's no part of my own purpose to follow West on this grand if rather woolly line although the historical treatment certainly throws up some interesting suggestions — for example, the rise of sentiment as the expression of a social sense other than the cash nexus that binds men in bourgeois society; and the decline of sentiment accompanying the decline of revolutionary ardour in nineteenth-century romanticism.

I take up West's discussion where he makes the point that though we long for social identification we feel that all emotions, ideas and words which touch the basic experience of social identification are associated with a system of society of which we cannot approve. On the other hand, we are not able to associate them with a system of society of which we can approve. Hence our suspicion of words like 'home', 'flag' and 'mother'. But, West says, Richards is wrong in suggesting that this inhibition of emotion is to be regretted. On the contrary: 'The loathing of sentimentality is a valuable defence against reactionary emotion, a positive assertion of new social ideals, however inarticulate, against the authority which deliberately appeals to emotion and feeling for its own ends.'

There are two interpolatory points I ought to make here. First, that the 'we' in West's argument is a group perfectly familiar in the 'thirties — those dissatisfied with bourgeois life but not yet communists. I don't know that a great many reading West today would identify with such a group but to my mind it matters not. It is plain that even on purely intellectual grounds — if there are such things — 'we' can reject the official ideas which attempt to hold 'our' society together. Secondly, though West is writing for an audience rejecting capitalism, unready for socialism, he himself is a committed Communist Party member, so that most of us would now find a certain crudity in his conclusions. For instance, after his point about the loathing of sentimentality being a defence against reactionary emotion he adds baldly: 'The weakness does not lie in rejecting bourgeois talk of the "flag" as sentimental, but in doing nothing to make it our flag.' But again, this seems to me not to detract from what he says on the way.

I want to hold on firmly to West's notion that the question of sentimentality is, as he says, bound up with the 'question of whether a man feels solidarity with a class he cannot believe in, or with a class he can believe in and work with'. At this stage in his argument, however, he takes a look at Richards's ideas which searches wider than the issue of sentimentality though bearing vitally upon it. Some people, Richards has observed, reject poetry partly because it violates the laws of nature. The reason for this rejection, he suggests, is the change from what he calls the magical view of the world to the scientific. It jars us to read of grass sighing and clouds holding monologues; and we become impatient with poetry if as we read it we have to keep science out of our mind. West has a number of objections to this reasoning. He says, for example, that 'the effect of science on the reading of poetry does not depend only on the intellectual relation between science and magic, but also on the relation of the reader to that social order of which the scientific control of nature will be the basis . . . There is no hostility between science and poetry, if one understands how to work for a social order where science will be a blessing . . . The feeling that science is in any way hostile to poetry, comes not from the nature of science itself, but from lack of faith in socialism.' We perhaps feel that West's simple political faith makes his expression at this moment rather naïve but he may well be right in thinking that a belief in socialism is a pre-requisite for a belief in the essential poeticality of science — the poeticality not only of science's ideal world but also of science's revelation of the existing world. Anyway, I would myself put the point less extremely and say that a poetry now that expressed hostility to science was in danger of sentimentality if only through its sacrifice of realism.

West's final words about Richards concern the relation of the poem to reality. Here, I think, he is not quite fair to Richards, possibly because of the brevity of the discussion. But in criticizing the notion that the poem is to be enjoyed on its own terms without reference to what the poet is saying about objective reality, West makes a point which has great relevance to my subject. 'There can be no poem', he says, 'and no response to a poem, without previous social activity. And that activity necessarily tests all utterances by their objective validity, because it is a matter of life and death to us whether what we say about the objective world is true or not. Our response to a poem derives from previous social activity; belief in our statements as truth, and not as myth, is an essential part of that activity. When Dr Richards wishes to preserve the emotional value of poetry by isolating it from beliefs about objective reality, he isolates it from the social activity which tests the objective truth of utterances by practice; he is destroying the possibility of any response to poetry by isolating the response from its only source.' It would lead me too far from my theme to pursue these questions, but I feel sure that here West is putting his finger on the cause of the uneasiness we often feel about Richards's concept of valuing a poem on its own terms.

Applying the arguments derived from West, therefore, we can expect the characteristics of sentimentality in poetry to express themselves in one or other or all of the following modes. First, reactionary emotion. Secondly, anti-scientific feeling. Thirdly, deficiency of realism. It is interesting and, I think, meaningful, that during the 'thirties a sentimental poetry was being incubated underneath the ideas that dominated 'thirties poetry — the commonsense ideas of Geoffrey Grigson, the Marxist ideas of critics like Alick West and Christopher Caudwell. When those ideas lost their dominance — by the end of the War, say, if one wants to put a date to it — the sentimental poetry broke the surface and gained recognition in a quite astonishing way. On the publication in 1946 of Dylan Thomas's collection *Deaths and Entrances*, I clearly remember being disconcerted by the proportion of pretentious and bogus work it contained, but this was in connection with Thomas's best vein. It never occurred to me that poems like 'Fern Hill' and 'Poem in October' would not only become popular but also receive critical acclaim.

And as I was green and carefree, famous among the barns
About the happy yard and singing as the farm was home . . .

Only a snatch of quotation is needed to remind one of the dilute Wordsworthianism of those pieces. They are sentimental because they are unrealistic about both the still-young poet recalling his childhood and that childhood itself; but, even more, they are sentimental because they bolster up the degenerate bourgeois notion of childhood as an idyll, a time of undifferentiated happiness, a memoried refuge from the unsatisfactoriness of adult life. One has only to open *The Prelude* to see the opposite qualities illustrated:

Sometimes it befell
In these night wanderings, that a strong desire
O'erpowered my better reason, and the bird
Which was the captive of another's toil
Became my prey; and when the deed was done
I heard among the solitary hills
Low breathings coming after me, and sounds
Of undistinguishable motion, steps
Almost as silent as the turf they trod.

As the 'forties succeeded the 'thirties, so the 'sixties succeeded the 'fifties. When the clear aims, logical thought, modest subject matter of the Larkins and the Thwaiteses became superannuated — as does every Movement when its members, past the first flush of youth, start to go their own ways and by no means always the ways of poetry — once more a poetry marked by sentimentality was let in. And again one finds an unrealistic and reactionary cult of the child. Here, from a poem by Brian Patten called 'Schoolboy', is a passage about the end of schooldays:

It is time to fathom out too many things.
To learn he's no longer got somebody watching over him;
he's going to know strange things, learn
how to lie correctly, how to lay correctly,
how to cheat and steal in the nicest possible manner.
He will learn amongst other things, how to enjoy
his enemies, and how to avoid friendships. If he's unlucky
he will learn how to love and give everything away
and how eventually, he'll end up with nothing.

The poem's irony here is inadequate, first because it assumes that a child's goodness issues from a condition of nature rather than the inheritance of a culture, and secondly because it discounts the possibility of adult rebellion against society's values. But today's sentimentality arises more characteristically from poetry about sexual love. From an embarrassment of examples I'll choose one which appears in a paperback anthology called *Love, love, love*: it is the start of a poem entitled 'Somewhere on the Way':

I wanted to say a lot of things:
I wanted to say how often lately
Your bright image has wandered through
The dusty old antique shop of my mind;
I wanted to say how good it is
To wake up in the morning
Knowing that the day contains
Something that is you.

No doubt it may be objected that this is merely an instance of indifferent poetry rather than of sentimentality resulting from inadequate realism. But it seemed right to choose the lines because their author, in his introduction to the anthology itself, implicitly claimed that the collection was a result of an 'increasing demand for living poetry, poetry that talks to people in a direct and comprehensible way', and shared the distinctive character of the poetry of the mid-'sixties — 'a vigour and feeling for the realities of life that have been absent from English poetry for too long'. Of course, these are claims that every new poetic movement is inclined to make, but here their foundations seem unusually frail. I should in fact have been quite able and willing to draw examples from rather older, more traditional and more officially respected poets:

> *I taught myself to name my name,*
> *To bark back, loosen love and crying:*
> *To ease my woman so she came.*

Those lines — which appear in the *Faber Book of Modern Verse* — I've long awaited the opportunity to quote, though whether their sentimentality results from their being unrealistic or anti-scientific I'd be gravelled to say. However, I thought it better on an occasion like this to take my examples from the really new, at the risk of seeming to be cracking nuts with a sledge-hammer.

One may well ask oneself at this point whether the attempted systematization of one's instincts about sentimentality is not after all merely a litmus paper for the detection of bad poetry which the process of time would anyway reject. My reply would be that quite apart from one's impatience with time as an arbiter of poetic merit, the long-term judgment of poetry has become bedevilled as a result of the poetic revolution at the end of the first decade of the century. It was this element in the question that I briefly referred to at the start.

> *One solace there is for me, sweet but faint,*
> *As it floats on the wind of the years,*
> *A whisper that spring is the last true thing*
> *And that triumph is born of tears.*

When Woodbine Willie's readers first came across those lines Swinburne had been dead only a few years. Except to a handful of specialists there was little chance of the poem's betraying itself by its lack of modernity. And when Richards exposed the poem to his students in the 'twenties its anonymity guaranteed its being placed for judgment in a stylistically appropriate period. Since 1910 stylistic changes have been frequent and compressed: moreover, through rapid communications and universal education those changes have been disseminated with remarkable completeness. The poet, particularly in recent times, has tended to be born as a fully fashionable being, without any slow period in the womb of himself developing through the gills and so forth of previous poetic modes. It is bound to be unlikely that a revolutionary turn brought about by a notable poet or group of poets will really serve the epigoni, so that true standards of achievement are often masked by an avant-garde form or diction. My favourite example of this comes from one of the self-styled 'Apocalyptic' poets of the 'forties who on one page of a collection had the early Dylan Thomas-ish line 'Swung from the ropes of his father's cackled rhyme' and on another:

> There is no sweeter sight, I swear, in Heaven
> Than blossoms on the cherry-tree by Clee.

Above all, I feel convinced of the value of the sentimentality test at a moment like the present which has seen such a remarkably widespread acceptance of the ideas about poetic form and diction that I suppose must be mainly associated with the American poet William Carlos Williams. In the England of the 'thirties Williams's American reputation was a puzzle. When in 1938 Julian Symons introduced an enterprising special American number of his magazine *Twentieth Century Verse* he had to admit that he did not understand Williams's poems at all. He appreciated in the poet a certain ironic simplicity of language but he was fogged completely by the text, that is to say insofar as he understood why it was that text and not some entirely different text. The poem that starts 'By the road to the contagious hospital' — even in those days quite celebrated — seemed to him 'a piece of second-hand and commonplace observation as might be turned out by any good poet on an off day'. And he ended by remarking that Williams's poems could not be imitated (nor would an imitation be attempted) by any Englishman. Symons did not reckon on the cocacolonization of English verse nor on the attractions of non-technique to a host of second-rate performers. It's scarcely too much to say that at present the cultural compulsion for a young poet to write in objectivist or projective verse is as strong as for a young painter to be an abstractionist.

'Objectivist or projective.' The former term, particularly associated with William Carlos Williams, is perhaps rather old-fashioned today. 'Projective verse', which I take describes the same thing, is a term invented I think by Charles Olson, the American poet and critic who taught at Black Mountain College, and is the one I shall use. The article Olson wrote about it in 1950 (available in James Scully's anthology *Modern Poets on Modern Poetry*) conveniently contains its recipes and claims. No doubt when one has read the article one has received nothing more concrete than a number of exhortations to write good verse; nevertheless a few rules or characteristics do emerge. A poem is to be constantly energetic and its form is to arise out of its content. The poet is to concentrate on the syllable rather than, for example, on metre and rhyme. The line must be kept from slowness, deadness, by being suspicious of description, of adjectives, of similes. The individual breath gives language its force, the force of speech, and insofar as the logical conventions of syntax hamper this force they must, in projective verse, go. The typewriter, because of its precision with spacing, is the personal and instantaneous recorder of the poet's work: with it he can indicate exactly the breath, the pauses, the suspensions — even of syllables — and the juxtapositions — even of parts of phrases — he intends.

Possibly this summary sounds arguable, even sensible in parts. It is true that I have left out Olson's tone of voice and very often it is the tone that first betrays the obsessed. For instance: 'I am dogmatic', Olson says, 'that the head shows in the syllable. The dance of the intellect is there, among them, in prose or verse. Consider the best minds you know in this here business: where does the head show, is it not, precise, here, in the swift currents of the syllable? can't you tell a brain when you see what it does, just there?' It's not my present purpose to polemicize against the theoretical justification of projective verse but if it were the sentimentalities of Olson's article would certainly need attention.

What I want to point out is the sanction given by projective verse to the typewriters and dubious breath of poets who would otherwise surely have remained utterly obscure. Even in a sincere and respectably-talented follower of Olson like Robert Creeley there is a dumbness that could only be tolerated in an art that allowed so much value to the instantaneous in thought and expression. Here is the start of his poem called 'For Love':

> Yesterday I wanted to
> speak of it, that sense above
> the others to me
> important because all
>
> that I know derives
> from what it teaches me.
> Today, what is it that
> is finally so helpless,
>
> different, despairs of its own
> statement, wants to
> turn away, endlessly
> to turn away.
>
> If the moon did not . . .
> no, if you did not
> I wouldn't either, but
> what would I not
>
> do, what prevention, what
> thing so quickly stopped.
> That is love yesterday
> or tomorrow, not
>
> now . . .

Such a poem is the thin end of the wedge which would encompass all the 'you knows', 'I means' and 'sort ofs' — not of ordinary speech (if, indeed, there is such a thing) but of a discourse of incoherent hints and inconclusiveness, a bewilderment in the face of emotion and of the real world; a discourse, needless to say, vulnerable to the grossest sentimentality. The point could be illustrated by opening almost at random almost any of the paperback collections whose recent publication in large editions has been thought by some to indicate a poetic revival. I will use volumes 12 and 13 of the Penguin Modern Poets. First, the start of a poem called 'just lately':

> *just lately*
> *I've seen through it*
> *I've seen through it all*
> *once, you know*
> *I was quite religious*
> *but now*
> *there is nothing, nothing*
> *yet still I pray . . .*

The second illustration is a complete poem:

ONE OF THOSE MORNINGS
& everything is suddenly a beautiful garden
with birds in it & angels & trees
> *made out of wings*
a crazy doodle of a garden
& you don't understand anything
> *but there you are*
making a poem of it
the most hopeless poem in the universe
> *oh god how my toe itches!*
that beautiful garden
> *friends*
> > *it is not there*

On the page that poem has a veneer of modernity that Woodbine Willie's lacks because of its ampersands, absence of punctuation and upper case, and its typewriter notation. Read aloud, it obviously has an 'instant' appeal to audiences too weary or too gormless to go through the business of grinding the beans and getting out the percolator. But its terms and attitude are, on the page, to me plainly inadequate, plainly sentimental.

I have tried so far to avoid basing my criticism on an examination of poetic language, though a poem's emotional and ideological deficiencies must in the end betray themselves in its vocabulary. In fact perhaps what worries us immediately in Woodbine Willie's stanza is the difficulty of apprehending what on earth the 'wind of the years' can be, and in Dylan Thomas's 'Poem in October' we may possibly be not too suspicious until we reach 'the sun of October/ *Summery*/ On the hill's shoulder'. But I've ignored language not least because sophisticated apologists for projective verse and the immense mass of more popular work it has engendered have sometimes admitted the unsatisfactoriness of its language while implying that this is more than compensated for in the freshness, genuineness and directness of its feeling. Thus Edward Lucie-Smith, in his introduction to the collection called *The Liverpool Scene*, said of the Liverpool poets that 'truth to feeling is valued much higher than truth to language'. My point of course is that the quality of the feeling determines the specific gravity of the poem equally with the quality of the language, if a separation of that kind is to be made.

i remember
i remember how
when you cried
the clouds cried too and the
streets became awash with tears

i remember
i remember how
when we lay together for the first time
the roomed smiled,
said: 'excuse-me',
and tiptoed away.
2*

If such Liverpudlian lines are to be tolerated except by a public similar to that which fifty years ago bought impression after impression of Woodbine Willie, doesn't it mean that *Practical Criticism* was written largely in vain? And isn't there all the more reason today for the more fundamental Westian approach to the business of sentimentality, an approach which must include not only the perennial problem of realism in art but also the question of poetry's allegiance to society's forces? More specifically, the superficially rebellious sort of poetry, frequently — and erroneously, it seems to me — tagged by middle-class critics 'working-class', operates quite profoundly to preserve the *status quo*. It operates thus in a number of disturbing ways. It is predisposed to a mid-Atlantic, tin pan alley language. It allies itself easily with tin pan alley entertainment. It exploits the indulgences and consolations of personal fantasies, particularly the sexual idealism characteristic of a literature content to exist on the periphery of the social questions that truly affect men's lives. It admits the unskilled and amateur practitioner because its disciplines have degenerated: it is therefore apt to persist as the poetry of a society moving towards the authoritarian and reactionary. In the modes of poetry's dissemination, particularly those reaching out to a newly-literate audience — the paperback, the gramophone record, the public reading — it tends to swamp the more serious and the more skilled: even worse, it begins to contaminate such work. How pathetic and uncomfortable it is to find at a public reading poets who should know better aiming to get the laughs and revolutionary frissons that they see achieved so effortlessly by their younger contemporaries. Finally, in the product of what may be called neo-spasmodic poets, needless to name and embarrassing to quote from, one sees sensationalism, violence and pornography taking over as they have taken over tracts of other departments of literature — with the usual effect not of spreading dissidence or insight but merely of selling what would otherwise have been the unsaleable to the unlettered. It might be of some comfort if one could say that this was a rot from a society sicker than ours but with the accident of a common language. However, the eager apostasy of British poets, the enthusiasm of their respectable apologists and the size of the audience they are finding forbid any self-righteousness.

I rather regret having used Woodbine Willie as a whipping boy. Unlike most of us he was a modest poet. When Richards asked his permission to employ his poem for the protocols in *Practical Criticism* he replied, though he must have known he was going to be exposed to a deal of obloquy: 'You can use any of my poems for any purpose you like. The criticisms of them could not be more adverse and slaughterous than my own would be.' In the light of such a remark the Woodbine Willies *de nos jours* seem all the more pretentious and dangerous.

III

An Artifice
of Versification

The origins of Marianne Moore's syllabic verse seem already lost in the mists of antiquity. Her first book was brought out without her knowledge in 1921 by her friends Bryher and the Imagist poet, H. D. She said later, in a characteristic phrase, that 'to issue my slight product — conspicuously tentative — seemed to me premature'. However, some time during the First World War she turned from a stress to a syllabic metre and evolved the extraordinary style that right up to the end of the 'thirties seemed likely to have no body of imitators, to remain a sport of English verse. She herself has denied that the style has literary antecedents.

But a few other poets in our time have experimented with syllabic counts. Above all I must mention Robert Bridges's daughter, Elizabeth Daryush. In the prefatory note to her *Verses*, Fourth Book, 1934, she defined what she meant — and what I mean here — by syllabic metres and the definition may be useful to those who are still uncertain what this lecture is going to be about. By syllabic metres she meant, she said, 'metres governed only by the number of syllables to the line, and in which the number and position of the stresses may be varied at will'. She distinguished her syllabic poems from the others by omitting line capitals, 'as a reminder', she said, 'to the reader to follow strictly the natural speech-rhythm, and not look for stresses where none are intended'. One might have thought that her syllabics were inspired by her father's investigations into Milton's blank verse and his own experiments in quantitative classical metres, but she points out in the note that the bulk of English so-called syllabic verse 'is, of course, not really syllabic in the strict sense, but more truly accentual', and she goes on to say some extremely interesting things on these lines. Moreover, she has written to me that she now realizes that her inclination towards the syllabic form goes back a very long way and that there were signs of it in her second verse collection, published in 1916, which she later suppressed — and that those signs came as a novelty to her father. I will return to Mrs Daryush's penetrating and practical remarks at later stages in the discussion. Whether, in the second decade of the century, Miss Moore ever saw and was influenced or reassured by Mrs Daryush's work I do not know. It seems unlikely. Certainly Mrs Daryush was not, she has told me, influenced by Miss Moore, who is still, to her, little more than a name. Like many revolutionary discoveries, the syllabic discovery seems to have been made contemporaneously but independently by separated workers in the same field. It is also an extraordinary coincidence that Mrs Daryush and Miss Moore were both born in the same year, 1887.

Ezra Pound, on seeing Marianne Moore's work originally, remarked: 'Someone has been reading Laforgue, and French authors.' But it was not Miss Moore, though retroactively she found the titles and treatment of Francis Jammes a good deal like her own. The fascinating technical discusssion that took place when Miss Moore was interviewed by Donald Hall for the *Paris Review* in 1960 did not disentangle syllabics from other innovations in her verse, such as her use of quotations, so we still have the tantalizing feeling that the last word on its parentage has not been said even by Miss Moore herself. Besides, her syllabic verse is quite dissimilar to literary devices, like the

fictional 'stream of consciousness', which can be traced to a work
or an author of little interest except as the embodiment of a
technical brainwave: Miss Moore's syllabics clothe a mind as well
as a considerable and individual poetic talent.

Pound himself never contemplated a metric based on a syllable
count. In a note of 1917 (which appeared in the *Pavannes and
Divisions* of 1918) he thought that in his own free verse he had
gone as far as was profitable towards looseness of stress, and
looked towards the authority and discipline of classical quantitative metres for possible further progress. Perhaps he had in mind
the experiments in this field of Bridges, to which I've already
referred, which had been appearing during the first two decades
of the century: certainly he had read Bridges as early as 1911.
The free verse of T. S. Eliot and of Arthur Waley, already
evolved by the time of the First World War, is, each in its
different way, based on stress, though Waley's was the more
revolutionary in the sense in which we are now thinking of
metrics since it was directed against the iambic line — one of his
exercises, he once said to me, was 'translating' the more Miltonic
passages of Wordsworth out of blank verse. Eliot made a number
of pronouncements about free verse in 1917 but his assumption
was — and I want to return to this interesting point later — that
free verse could always be *scanned*. No doubt the technical freedom
of Imagist poetry gave some sanction for the practices of Miss
Moore's early verse, but one looks in vain in the work of her
friend H.D., say, for anything like Mooreish syllabics. In the
non-syllabic poem of Miss Moore's he quoted in his introduction
to her 1935 *Selected Poems*, Eliot saw 'a slight influence' of H.D.
but really this seems confined to the one word 'splintered'. The
truth of the matter is that Imagism was 'a theory about the
use of material', as Eliot said in 1917, and not a theory about
metrics.

The short poem quoted by Eliot, 'A Talisman', deviates from
strict stress metre merely in having a couple of rhymes on weak
syllables:

Under a splintered mast,
torn from the ship and cast
            near her hull,

a stumbling shepherd found
embedded in the ground,
            a sea-gull . . .

This is a practice that only becomes really interesting and meaningful, I think, when regular stress has disappeared, as in Miss Moore's later verse. However, the poem is amusingly prophetic in another way in that it shows interest in one of the few aspects of stress metre where the single syllable is vital — that is, at the start of an iambic line shorter than the pentameter. It is worth adding here a remark of Elizabeth Daryush in the prefatory note to her book *The Last Man and Other Verses* 'that when (in fully-rhymed "syllabic" verse) a line has a feminine ending, I mean it to be regarded as ending with a monosyllabic unaccented rhyme, and not (as might sometimes be thought) with a disyllabic half-rhyme'. The point is obvious now, but it presumably wasn't so as late as 1936, when this book was published.

In characterizing Miss Moore's mature verse critics usually describe her elaborately arranged stanza, with its indented lines of varying numbers of syllables and its one or two rhymes — the stanza of 'The Steeple-Jack', say:

Dürer would have seen a reason for living
      in a town like this, with eight stranded whales
to look at; with the sweet sea air coming into your house
on a fine day, from water etched
      with waves as formal as the scales
on a fish.

An odd thing is that the stanza's syllabic count — in this case 11, 10, 9, 8, 8, 3 — is not strictly maintained through the poem. This can be detected not by the ear, only by the fingers, but it rather threatens the foundations of what, though primarily a discipline for the poet, is for the reader authorized by ingenuity and symmetry. My own feeling is that the reader's confident expectation of a regular mathematical pattern ought not, if initially offered, to be destroyed by the writer of syllabic verse, but that it can be destroyed and that Miss Moore herself sometimes destroys it has a bearing, as I shall mention later, on the validity of the technique. Again, between the 1935 *Selected Poems* and the 1951 *Collected Poems* three and a half lines disappeared from a poem called 'The Buffalo'. Miss Moore merely replaced them with a row of dots, thereby mangling the shape of two stanzas.

Elizabeth Daryush, in the 1934 note I've quoted from already, put with characteristic precision the feeling about syllabic counts that I've just expressed. She was talking about elisions — and it seems to me that in this matter, too, she was absolutely right and that some other syllabic practitioners, including Auden, are not right. In syllabic metres, she said: 'I make it a rule to allow no elisions except those that are natural, unavoidable, *and complete* in ordinary deliberate speech. (For instance, the semi-vowels before the final consonant in *heaven, chasm,* &c, are only elided when followed by another vowel, and even then only under certain conditions of the speech-rhythm. Such words, therefore, in general, I reckon as disyllables.) In accentual verse the metre demands and justifies the use both of optional and incomplete elisions, but these are obviously out of place in a purely syllabic system. The fact that any ambiguity of this sort would be fatal to it, implies the reduction of the syllabic units to their limit, so as to prevent any uncertainty in the mind of the reader with regard to their further reduction.' I shall have a further brief word about elision later.

I must be fair here and refer to a tape-recorded conversation that Miss Moore had with Grace Schulman in 1967, transcribed in numbers 1–2 of volume xvi of the *Quarterly Review of Literature* in 1969. On that occasion Miss Moore said of 'the syllabic method', 'Oh, I just hate that!' But this remark is rather like Marx

denying that he was a Marxist. Miss Moore went on to say: 'I
suppose I do, after the thing is done, count the syllables, to know
how nearly I have followed a set example in the second stanza
from the first, but I never possibly could think of it until *after*
I had written it. Then you see how mathematically it comes
out . . .' I think myself that Miss Moore is recounting here no
more than the experience that a mere tyro in syllabic verse-
writing can have, that even the dashed-down first draft can
approximate to the required syllabic pattern: Miss Moore's own
rider is that she isn't too fussy about absolute replication of the
pattern. 'For instance,' she said, 'in "My Crow Pluto" I set
myself to write stanzas of two lines with two syllables in each . . .
And I tried to continue it all the way through. I didn't succeed,
but I had it in mind.' She was then asked if she could hear the
number of syllables in a line without counting them. 'Oh yes,'
she said, 'I don't think about the mathematics of it at all.' I
fancy that her interlocutor was sceptical about this or at any rate
thought it needed amplification, for later in the conversation she
repeated the question, saying that in French it is possible to hear
the number of syllables, but that English was a stressed language.
'Can you really hear them?' Miss Moore was pressed. 'Can the
reader hear them?' I'm sorry to report that Miss Moore ducked
the question this second time round, though her answer is
interesting and bears on something I shall be raising a little later.
She said: 'At first, I never realized until we got tape recorders and
records that the spoken line is different from the one on the page
sometimes. And then I tried to read out loud what I'd written,
and then I saw I would have to alter a good deal. Some of the
lines wouldn't read, and I revised a number of things. I found that
in reading a thing aloud you have to change the wording.'

However, moving away from this question, I think it has been
insufficiently emphasized that a good deal of Miss Moore's verse,
particularly the earlier, is not stanzaic at all, or rhymed — or,
indeed, regularly, or approximately regularly, syllabic. Nevertheless, perhaps it is here that her contribution to modern experi-
mental poetry may be seen at its purest and most remarkable, for

what she is writing is not prose or the prose-poem but poetry with prose's rhetoric, complexity and ease, poetry without adventitious musical aid, whose units are arguments and paragraphs. I quote the second half of the poem 'Snakes, Mongooses, Snake Charmers and the Like', a passage about the snake:

Thick, not heavy, it stands up from its travelling-basket,
the essentially Greek, the plastic animal all of a piece from nose to tail;
one is compelled to look at it as at the shadows of the alps
imprisoning in their folds like flies in amber, the rhythms of the
*   skating-rink.*
This animal to which from the earliest times, importance has attached,
fine as its worshippers have said — for what was it invented?
To show that when intelligence in its pure form
has embarked on a train of thought which is unproductive, it will
*   come back?*
We do not know; the only positive thing about it is its shape; but
*   why protest?*
The passion for setting people right is in itself an afflictive disease.
Distaste which takes no credit to itself is best.

Of course, in such a passage two things must be immediately remarked. First, a good many of the long lines are end-stopped, so that the technique seems Whitmanesque rather than particularly Mooreish. And secondly, much of it can be scanned, in Eliot's sense — the last line, for example, is a perfect alexandrine.

When, as we may on disc, we hear Miss Moore reading her poetry — and I am specifically referring now to that written in complex stanzas — we may at first find the experience surprising. For the rapid, rather nasal voice pays no attention to line endings even when they rhyme, and the syllables that have been counted out with (more or less) painstaking accuracy are often slurred over. (It is true that in the Schulman conversation Miss Moore said, 'I can hardly bear the recordings when I hear them. I say "plenny" for "plenty", and "granmother" for "grandmother". I'm trying not to.' But this doesn't destroy the point I'm making). However, it soon becomes apparent that she is reading for sense and, of course, this is how she must be read on the page: the baroque cleverness and ornament is to delay and enrich a closely-argued journey towards the clinching spire or altar of meaning and emotion. The experience of the records is borne out by the Schulman conversation where Miss Moore agreed that the reader (including the reader of the printed page) shouldn't pause after the line-breaks. 'The actual punctuation,' she said, 'tells you where to pause' — though she made the typically Mooreish qualification 'that sometimes you want emphasis, as if you were stopping, and couldn't go on any further.' But presumably such an effect with a line-ending could only be gained on the page — or, at a reading aloud, by the poet herself. And as to the *look* of Miss Moore's poems on the page — often such a striking feature — she insisted, obviously rightly, that this, the visual pattern was 'not at all as important' as the spoken one; 'although', she added, 'I do think of it. I like to see symmetry on the page, I will confess.' And she emphasized that if she breaks the pattern she has set it is in the interests of natural speech. 'I don't want it artificial,' she said, 'and it ought to be continuous . . . I like to have it all natural and consecutive, no matter how it counts on the page.'

Miss Moore has said more than once that what she writes can only be called poetry because there is no other category in which to put it. Up to the last war there was a sense in which such a statement might have commanded assent in that she was for all practical purposes the sole practitioner of the technique she had invented (or obscurely evolved) — a Schoenberg without disciples. But in the Winter 1940 *Kenyon Review*, W. H. Auden printed his poem 'In Memory of Sigmund Freud' whose four-line unrhymed stanzas were in the syllabic pattern 11,11,9,10.

When there are so many we shall have to mourn,
When grief has been made so public, and exposed
   To the critique of a whole epoch
   The frailty of our conscience and anguish,

Of whom shall we speak? For every day they die
Among us, those who were doing us some good,
And knew it was never enough but
    Hoped to improve a little by living.

This poem, of which I have quoted the first two stanzas, was reprinted in the collection of Auden's poems called *Another Time* (first published on February 7, 1940) and must obviously have been written soon after Freud's death in September 1939. It has been pointed out to me that another poem in *Another Time*, the rhymed piece later regrettably called 'Heavy Date', also sticks rigidly to a syllabic pattern, though it is possible to read it as a stressed poem. Here the eight-line stanzas have a syllabic pattern of 6,6,6,5,6,6,6,5, the two shorter lines rhyming. I quote one of them:

Sharp and silent in the
Clear October lighting
Of a Sunday morning
    The great city lies;
And I at a window
Looking over water
At the world of Business
    With a lover's eyes.

I have also been reminded that some earlier poems by Auden are printed in their latest versions without initial capitals to the lines, as though they were to be read syllabically, but that their looseness and odd enjambments are more related to the freedom of form of 'Spain' and the 'Epilogue' to *Look, Stranger*, a freedom which goes back to *The Orators*. We know from Auden's book of essays, *The Dyer's Hand*, that when in 1935 he first tried to read Miss Moore's poems he 'simply could not make head or tail of them'. Clearly on his going to live in America closer acquaintance with the poetry or the poet prompted him to adopt the Mooreish style and it has since been a most important influence on his manner — and I mean by that the totality of the poetic effect, for obviously though poetic technique may be isolated for the purposes of discussion it is inseparable from poetry's content. Moreover, through Auden's authority and popularity, syllabic metres have become a freely available procedure, used by many poets as a change from stress metres or free verse based on stress, and indeed by some as a normal mode of composition. It would be quite unjust if I didn't emphasize here that, long before Auden, Elizabeth Daryush had thought, as she said in the 1934 note, that on a strict syllabic system 'it should be possible to build up subtler and more freely-followed accentual patterns than can be obtained either by stress-verse proper, or by the traditional so-called syllabic metres'. Had her own verse been more flamboyant it must surely have led to the system catching on in England independently of the delay in Miss Moore's publication over here, and of Auden's example.

It has a bearing on the general viability of syllabic metre that for Miss Moore herself its convenience must have been brought home or consolidated by her practice of incorporating extracts from prose works into her poetry. Needless to speculate whether chicken or egg came first, but certainly the extreme extent of the practice in her case presupposes a syllabic basis for the poetry's metrics. One may assume, too, though this is a far less vital matter, that her device of isolating the first line of a poem, or part of it, as the title was prompted by a necessity or convenience in the arithmetic of regular syllabics. I add here a note from my own experience. I was once asked by the editor of *The London Magazine* to bring back a poem from a holiday in Spain. I can never write away from home but I returned with a few observations which seemed to engage with some ideas in or about Henry James's novel *The Bostonians* which I'd read on holiday. However, despite a good deal of trying the thing wouldn't go at all in rhymed or even blank or blankish verse. Then I bethought myself of syllabic metre, though previously I'd never used it except as a deliberate exercise in a short poem for children. The poem immediately got itself written, not least because I was able to incorporate extracts from James's prose in the second of the two opening stanzas, both of which perhaps I may read:

At the next table, on the terrace
(The Bostonians open on my
Knee) a pale pumice domineering
Head; in the prosperous buttonhole
An order. Behind the lush hotel,
Folds of burnt-brown, donkey-littered hills,
Beyond which runs the river with the
Battle-name. Old man, did you, thirty
Years ago, fire the shot that killed my friend?

'Whatever money was given her
She gave it away to a negro
Or a refugee. No woman could
Be less invidious, but on the
Whole she preferred these two classes of
The human race.' Though even Henry
Found history grave at last, came to
The 'unspeakable give-away of
The whole fool's paradise of our past.'

Of course for most poems and most poets the advantage of syllabic verse in accommodating prose quotations does not apply. The use of the technique, if not dictated by mere fashion, must reside in providing an escape from iambic clichés, a chance of making a fresh music. From the poet's point of view, as I can testify, the technique can provide a way into the composition of a poem, particularly at the dry start of a period of poetic productiveness, by freeing him from the preliminary need to hear his subject, his *donnée*, his initial observation or image, as song — or at least the often elusive song of traditional stress metre. No doubt this is due partly to the fundamentally simpler mathematics of syllabic metre, partly to the closeness in tone and rhythm of the finished poem to its prosaic origins. As to the bypassing of the iambic — and, indeed, other stress rhythms that may be felt to be outworn — it seems to me curious that Miss Moore (and Auden following her) does not avoid writing in lines of an even number of syllables. Even numbers tend to the iambic. In the stanza form of Miss Moore's poem 'A Carriage from Sweden', for example, four of its five lines are eight syllables long, and the poem starts like this:

> They say there is a sweeter air
> where it was made, than we have here;
> a Hamlet's castle atmosphere.
> At all events there is in Brooklyn
> something that makes me feel at home.

Despite the regular internal rhymes, the impression left here is of iambic tetrameter gone lame in the metre — because of the nine-syllable fourth line — and in the rhyme scheme. (Perhaps the iambics have caused the lapse in the third line, for surely the reference should be to Macbeth's castle.) This impression is reinforced by the second stanza and revived later in the poem although many of the stanzas are not end-stopped. Particularly unsatisfactory is the eighth stanza where Miss Moore, it must be through a First Form arithmetical slip despite what she has said about breaking the pattern, gives nine syllables to the fifth line as well:

> The puzzle-jugs and hand-spun rugs,
> the root-legged kracken shaped like dogs,
> the hanging buttons and the frogs
> that edge the Sunday jackets! Sweden,
> you have a runner called the Deer, who . . .

It seems obvious to me that the metrical effect Miss Moore was really aiming for is shown, for example, by the fourth stanza of the poem:

> Seats, dashboard and sides of smooth gourd-
> rind texture, a flowered step, swan-
> dart brake, and swirling crustacean-
> tailed equine amphibious creatures
> that garnish the axletree! What . . .

It is significant how in the first stanza of this poem the regular iambics have led to a certain flabbiness and sentimentality uncharacteristic of the writer, particularly the line 'something that makes me feel at home'. One finds the same weakness elsewhere when the iambic accidentally cuts across the syllabic lines, particularly where it is emphasized by strong rhymes. There is an instance in the celebrated war-time poem 'In Distrust of Merits', which in any case hovers on the edge of over-plus feeling: 'O/ quiet form upon the dust, I cannot/ look and yet I must.' The rest of the stanza, purely syllabic, in which those lines occur seems to me far more acceptable:

> . . . *The world's an orphans' home. Shall*
> *we never have peace without sorrow?*
> *without pleas of the dying for*
> *help that won't come? O*
> *quiet form upon the dust, I cannot*
> *look and yet I must. If these great patient*
> *dyings — all these agonies*
> *and wound-bearings and bloodshed —*
> *can teach us how to live, these*
> *dyings were not wasted.*

An equally instructive example of the damaging effect of the iambic occurs in the last lines of the poem 'Nevertheless' — 'What sap/ went through that little thread/ to make the cherry red!' I don't think the word 'little' is well-judged at this point but I have no doubt that it is the fortuitous iambic that softens up an otherwise unexceptionable observation.

Less frequently some metre even more inappropriate than the iambic accidentally intrudes, as in the poem called 'The Jerboa': 'Its leaps should be set/ to the flageolet.' As twelve-tone music must avoid the old concord, so — with, as I think, more sense — syllabics must in general avoid regular stress, certainly any stress pattern that calls attention to itself, as do the anapaests of my last example. An exercise of Miss Moore's like the little poem 'To a Prize Bird', made up of eight and ten syllable lines that also scan precisely according to stress, seems rather wasted. Here is the first stanza:

You suit me well; for you can make me laugh,
nor are you blinded by the chaff
that every wind sends spinning from the rick.

However, this was an early poem, perhaps a milestone on the way to the evolution of the fully syllabic style. Many of Mrs Daryush's poems, too, scan both on syllabic and on accentual principles, as she points out in the 1934 note. And I must add that though she, too, works in even numbers of syllables, she is much more alert than Miss Moore in escaping the pitfalls I've referred to.

It may well be thought, particularly by those who are not practising poets, that the essential arbitrariness and faint absurdity of syllabic counting puts the method quite out of court. Plainly I don't believe this is necessarily so. For one thing, when one works in lines of an odd number of syllables one is working at what seems to be a logical extension of the problems of the normal metrical English line. Behind the eleven-syllable line, for example, is the ghost of the iambic pentameter, but the constant intrusion of just one extra syllable — the exercise of accommodating it — removes the sense there is about blank verse that its possibilities of variation have already been exhausted, or at any rate discovered, by the great practitioners of the past. A syllabic heroic couplet might similarly be experimented with: indeed, in his translations of Molière Richard Wilbur inserted an occasional extra-syllabled line obviously to try to avoid the archaic glibness that to our ears is a drawback of this form. But so far as unrhymed syllabics are concerned I would not personally be worried that the iambic might accidentally result — though, as may be seen from Miss Moore's verse, one has to be on guard for the too-resounding coinciding with the highly emotional. No doubt syllabics tend to impose too many merely arbitrary and feminine line-endings, but here again the practitioner, as is the case with stress metres, will keep his eye on end-stopping, both in lines and in stanzas. It seems to me that the sense of aptness, even of triumph, in achieving the right proportion of end-stopping works with syllabic metres as with stress metres, perhaps more so. Mrs Daryush's poetry repays study in this respect. And probably with syllabics it is the stanza or the paragraph rather than the line which is the unit in this business: certainly one has the feeling that at least the virtues of good syllabic verse are the virtues of good prose, and I, for one, would always place confidence in a poet who, like Miss Moore, composed and read verse for sense.

I've singled out Miss Moore's as the ur-syllabic verse, and Auden as the Prometheus who has made it available to the general. But of course there exists a different, more mystical and less arithmetical syllabic verse, particularly that associated with the practice of William Carlos Williams and the theory of Charles Olson. That verse, as I have said on a previous occasion, has in my view provided a sanction for much that is now being written — metrical really in no sense — which lacks the authority of a serious practitioner like Williams and even of a critic like Olson, vague and misguided though I consider him to be. It was just about 200 years ago that Dr Johnson remarked that he had not been troubled for a long time with authors desiring his opinion of their works. He was not, of course, the occupant of this Chair. He added: 'I used once to be plagued with a man who wrote verses, but who literally had no other notion of a verse, but that it consisted of ten syllables. *Lay your knife and your fork across your plate*, was to him a verse:

$$- \quad - \quad - \quad - \quad -$$

Lay your knife and your fork, across your plate.
As he wrote a great number of verses, he sometimes by chance made good ones, though he did not know it.' One sympathizes with Johnson — of whom T. S. Eliot is but a modern extension — in his view that mere syllables make prose not poetry, but I fear it is too simple-minded.

One can't help being aware at this point of one's sense that though contributing to it for more than 40 years one has never had a real grasp of English prosody. It is a nebulous, indeed awe-inspiring subject that perhaps awaits for completer and less quirky delineation critics with the discoveries of the computer

at their minds' ends. I will just mention, and leave hurriedly
behind, the strange and fascinating question of the prosody of
Paradise Lost. There seems no doubt that this is Lay-your-knife-
and-your-fork-across-your-plate verse. Milton was working on
a fundamental line of ten syllables. As is often Auden's way with
syllabic verse — and occasionally Miss Moore's, too: what, in
the Schulman conversation, she called grace notes — elisions
and contractions based on speech practice have to be taken into
account when doing the syllabic sum. An example educed by
Alastair Fowler in his and John Carey's superb edition of Milton,
is 'Till, as a signal given, the uplifted spear.' 'Given' must be con-
tracted to a monosyllable and the definite article is run into the
ensuing verb — 'th'uplifted'. One result is, of course, that the
Miltonic so-called blank verse line may have as few as three
stresses. 'Lay your knife and your fork across your plate', having
four stresses, would have gone unremarked into *Paradise Lost*.
I should say that Mrs Daryush, in the 1934 note, is in no doubt
that Milton's blank verse is essentially accentual in character, for
her conclusively proved (interestingly enough) by the very
exceptions and licences Milton allows in the syllabic count. The
question of how far quantity, in the Latin sense, entered into
Milton's calculations, critics in general — even Robert Bridges —
have failed to grapple with, as Alastair Fowler points out. No
wonder. Another interesting question, it seems to me, is whether
the bad, anti-everyday speech influence of Milton on English
verse after him had anything to do with his conceiving the over-
powering example of *Paradise Lost* in syllabic rather than stress
terms. And further, whether a body of work in syllabics, like
Marianne Moore's and Auden's, may have some similar dele-
terious effect in the future. Certainly Auden's later style — like
Henry James's later style, sometimes giving the effect of picking
up peas with boxing-gloves — is intimately connected with his
syllabic practice. It is a curious paradox of syllabic verse that
though the escape from regular stress in theory brings one closer
to speech rhythms (as Mrs Daryush noted), nevertheless the
greater freedom leads easily to greater complexity of diction.

Apropos of what I said earlier, I ought to refer here to Milton's use of the eleven-syllable line, though I think it was an experiment confined to the terminal syllable — 'The fruitless hours, but neither self-condemning.' (Elizabeth Daryush argues for his usage of an *initial* extra syllable also, but a discussion of this would show up my amateurishness on the subject even more.) The thing is sparsely used and rightly so, otherwise Milton would have had the problem of the ubiquitous feminine ending on his hands. And as to end-stopping, one recalls Dr Johnson's reactionary but thought-provoking view of the verse of *Paradise Lost*. He remarked, in his life of the author, that 'There are only a few skilful and happy readers of Milton, who enable their audience to perceive where the lines end or begin. "Blank verse", said an ingenious critick, "seems to be verse only to the eye." ' However, I think we must admit that Milton's success with the run-over line — which all have acclaimed as one of the prime greatnesses of his blank verse — resulted precisely from his conceiving the iambic pentameter as syllabic. As the American critic Yvor Winters once said: 'In the standard metres, the run-over line tends to be awkward because of the heavy rhythmic pause at the end of each line.' Winters also pointed out that in Milton the device of enjambment is 'a basis for sensitive modulations of rhetoric'. So Marianne Moore and Auden have found to be their syllabics.

I was uneasily conscious as I prepared this lecture of some preliminary remarks made by A. E. Housman when he delivered the Leslie Stephens Lecture at Cambridge on 9th May 1933. His subject was, of course, 'The Name and Nature of Poetry' but he said that he had first thought of taking for his theme 'The Artifice of Versification'. This was a subject, he added, 'that has underlying it a set of facts which are unknown to most of those who practise it; and their success, when they succeed, is owing to instinctive tact and a natural goodness of ear. This latent base, comprising natural laws by which all versification is conditioned, and the secret springs of the pleasure which good versification can give, is little explored by critics: a few pages of Coventry

Patmore and a few of Frederic Myers contain all, so far as I know, or all of value, which has been written on such matters; and to these pages I could add a few more. But they would not make a good lecture: first, because of their fewness; secondly, because of their dryness; and thirdly, because they might not be easy for listeners to follow.'

In the printed text of the lecture there is a remarkable footnote to this passage in which Housman lists some of the natural laws at the basis of versification with which he might have dealt had he recklessly risked boring his audience and taken that for his subject. They were: 'the existence in some metres, not in others, of an inherent alternation of stresses, stronger and weaker; the presence in verse of silent and invisible feet, like rests in music; the reason why some lines of different length will combine harmoniously while others can only be combined by great skill or good luck; why, while blank verse can be written in lines of ten or six syllables, a series of octosyllables ceases to be verse if they are not rhymed; how Coleridge, in applying the new principle which he announced in the preface to Christabel, has fallen between two stools; the necessary limit to the inversion of stress, which Milton understood and Bridges overstepped; why, of two pairs of rhymes, equally correct and both consisting of the same vowels and consonants, one is richer to the mental ear and the other poorer; the office of alliteration in verse, and how its definition must be narrowed if it is to be something which can perform that office and not fail of its effect or actually defeat its purpose.'

In a brilliantly hostile review of *The Name and Nature of Poetry* which appeared in the *Criterion* soon after the publication of the lecture, Ezra Pound pointed out the limitations of Housman's reading on the subject of versification. Even in Housman's day — that is, his day as a practising poet — there were Bridges and Hopkins. And later there were Eliot and Pound himself — to say nothing of poetries other than English. But Pound, with his characteristic generosity, said of the footnote previously quoted that it was 'one of the most masterly summaries of a small section of the problems of metric that I have ever had the pleasure to come on. I doubt if anyone has done anything better in English, that is to say, listed a larger number of more important — some of them possibly fundamental issues, in so small a compass.'

I have appealed to the authority of Pound in reminding you of the vital and continuing puzzles of traditional metres not least because his name is often invoked by those who maintain that those metres are now unusable. My own instinct and experience leads me to believe that the syllabic verse which is viable in English is in the last analysis an extension of more traditional metres, not a denial of them. Certainly syllabic verse has its own advantages, some of which I have tried to delineate. Equally certainly, it seems to me, its procedures do not somehow provide an escape from the considerations, such as Housman specified, of traditional verse. I would add, too, that the great weight of tradition has a pull which the poet who has been gambolling in the comparative weightlessness of syllabics will resist at his peril. The return to tradition will be all the more effective after a regimen of syllabics has reinforced his conviction of the importance of a direct word order and renewed his consciousness of the possibility, the necessity, of speech tones in verse.

The heresy of syllabic verse in English resides in its evolution as mere chopped-up prose; in its so-called typewriter notation; and in its unjustified imitation of more highly inflected languages. As to this last, my sense is that a great part of the American fashion for syllabic verse, now such a large import here, arises from an imperfect notion of traditional English verse possessed by Americans whose parents spoke — or themselves spoke — another language. And in this connection I see a danger in the often literal translations from modern poets now so widely circulating in paperback and which I suspect frequently provide young English poets with a model and a sanction. But without the aid of our own verse traditions, the force, the smartness, the epigrammatic quality of highly inflected languages can usually only be transferred to English via a souped-up violence or some anti-poetical notation on the page.

In saying this I must not be taken to mean that English verse is not still capable of being enriched by foreign influence: on the contrary. But the enrichment must come about through the practice of considerable poets. On this subject I would adopt much of what Eliot once said in a lecture called 'The Music of Poetry', and his remarks are also germane to the place of syllabics in the English tradition. Eliot was somewhat too sceptical about the possibility of evolving rules from the practice of English metrics, as well as being always rather comically deprecating about his own knowledge of the subject. Doubtless this was part of his strategy — and all good critics (I try to tell myself) must evolve such a strategy to avoid a barren and limiting dogmatism — to keep from too violent a conclusion on literary matters. But one modest aperçu in 'The Music of Poetry' seems to me extraordinarily helpful in a difficult area. After mentioning the view of some classical scholars 'that the native measure of Latin poetry was accentual rather than syllabic, that it was overlaid by the influence of a very different language — Greek', he went on to say that he could not help suspecting 'that to the cultivated audience of the age of Virgil, part of the pleasure in the poetry arose from the presence in it of two metrical schemes in a kind of counterpoint: even though the audience may not necessarily have been able to analyse the experience. Similarly, it may be possible that the beauty of some English poetry is due to the presence of more than one metrical structure in it.' It would have been interesting if he had gone on to place his admiration for Marianne Moore's poetry in this context.

I might add here an observation by Graham Hough from his thoughtful 1957 Warton Lecture on 'Free Verse'. He said that 'in conventionally metrical verse there are always two rhythms at work, one provided by the ideal metrical norm, whatever it is, the other by the syntactic structure; while in free verse there is only one, that provided by the syntactic structure.' He added that the powerful effects of traditional verse gained by playing off the syntactical movement against the metrical movement are closed to free verse since there is no metrical norm to appeal to. I think we must allow that the main movement of Mooreish syllabic verse is syntactical and that the movement against which it is played off — the regular count of syllables — exists more as an intellectual element than an aural one. Hough might find its limitation in this respect no less than that of free verse, and certainly he would regard the great bulk of verse authorized by Olson as having the narrower scope of chopped-up prose. Nevertheless, as I have tried perhaps not very clearly to suggest, the counter of syllables is, even in the act of waggling his fingers, bound to be conscious in some way of stress — though often it may be no more than the low thrum of a comparatively unimportant ground bass.

I end by insisting, in the field of syllabic verse, on Miss Moore's example of marvellous elaboration. Yvor Winters once said, rightly I think, that the nature of free verse was an obstacle to complexity and profundity. No such objection can be made to syllabic verse, at least in the hands of Mrs Daryush, Miss Moore and Auden. Whatever the poet may consciously know or not know about the techniques of his craft; how far such things are mysteries or natural laws or capable of explanation; whatever the extent to which English prosody may admit new rules, new practices — one thing is certain: there is nothing particularly simple about the way good poems are fabricated. I can think of no better words in which to sum up my conviction of the matter than these by the American poet and critic Allen Tate, whose own fine work demonstrates that there need be no despair about the tradition of English poetry wherever it may be written and written about: 'Formal versification is the primary structure of poetic order, the assurance to the reader and to the poet himself that the poet is in control of the disorder both outside him and within his own mind.' It is hardly necessary for me to add that it is syllabic verse's extreme formal element that above all else gives one confidence in its validity.

POSTSCRIPT

Part of this lecture derived from a lecture given at the Royal Society of Literature in 1968 and from a review in *The Times Literary Supplement* of Marianne Moore's *Complete Poems*. When I was rearranging and adding to this material I was vaguely conscious of the work of Elizabeth Daryush but merely mentioned her as a poet who had used syllabics. Not long before the lecture was delivered I felt guilty at not having made a more thorough investigation and was thus led to Mrs Daryush's penetratingly clear writings on the subject now referred to in the lecture. I also looked at more of her poetry and realized that I was quite wrong in what I had previously carelessly assumed — that her experiments were mainly confined to combining a regular syllabic count with regular stress. Since Mrs Daryush had published no book in England after 1938 and having regard to the year of her birth, 1887, it was an added pleasure to find that she was still a practising poet.

She has kindly given me permission to quote from the reply to a letter I wrote to her asking if her syllabics had been inspired by Robert Bridges and whether there were any links between her and Miss Moore. I refer to this in the lecture but I think it will be useful to have the *ipsissima verba*. 'It is hardly correct', she wrote, 'to say that my syllabic ventures were "inspired by" my father's "investigations into Milton's blank verse, and his own experiments in classical metres." I now realise that my inclination towards this form goes back a very long way. In my second collection (1916) a distinctly childish production which I have since suppressed, there are obvious signs of it . . . However, my approach, in direct contrast to [my father's] own, has never been deliberately technical. What rules I have arrived at are the result of an almost unconscious analysis of my dissatisfaction, or otherwise, with what I have already (again half subconsciously) written. And despite his often expressed opinion, by which I have no doubt been influenced, that the traditional "accentual syllabics"

3

were, as he put it "played out", and his life-long interest in technical possibilities, I think that perhaps he never quite appreciated the full implication of a whole-hearted surrender to the syllabic principle — as, for instance, in the use of unaccented rhymes, and the strict avoidance of all ambiguity in the matter of elision.

'Owing to failing eyesight, my knowledge of modern verse is minimal — Marianne Moore is little more than a name to me — apart from one or two casual perusals in anthologies I know nothing of her work.'

From a subsequent conversation I had with Mrs Daryush I believe she would agree with me in finding a particular interest in the odd-numbered syllabic line. In one of her recent poems she actually uses the eleven-syllable line (in conjunction with ten- and twelve-syllable lines).

I am also indebted to Father Peter Levi for letting me quote the following extracts from a personal letter he wrote to me after hearing my lecture. I do so because he so clearly indicates some lines of further investigation open to those with the scholarly qualifications I lack myself.

'I have been looking up the preface to Christabel; it's important for Hopkins (not centrally, but still important) isn't it? Of course the concern with metre and how to record or count it is general in English 19th century poets, at least so I suppose, and of course Bridges read everything, but his daughter is an interesting late stage of the movement.

'I wondered though if you didn't neglect two things, the Italian background of Milton's prosody, which I think goes a long way to explain it, and the fact that metre is cumulative in its effect, so that the effect of variations is carried over (as in multiplication sums) from line to line, or even stanza to stanza, beyond the limits of what seems the metrical unit.

'The point about classical metres is deducible if not clearly stated in primers of verse composition in Latin: it is a fault and an impossibility to have a line like "fortia corpora fudit Aias" in which stress and quantity coincide. Even Homer is known to have used words of which the natural quantity is altered by his metres, as in singing (perhaps it *was* sung). Incidentally did you know that with words that alter their quantity in the process of time, Virgil masks the syllable of which he's doubtful (Pollio et ipse canit) by elision, though Ovid accepts the new pronunciation? In Horace, in odes 4, 5, you get echoes of a rhythmic, stress-scanned street-cry built into a quantitative metre.

'As for the English application, I have been assuming for many years that the ictus of English poetry depends on a tension between quantitative and stress patterns, but that both ought to be carefully considered. The only difference is that in Latin the quantity and in English the stress is uppermost. But

⏑ _ ⏑   ⏑ _   ⏑⏑ _⏑⏑ _

'Sir Hiram he robed him in ghostly attire" is as bad as "fortia corpora fudit Aias" because stress and quantity correspond. Interesting that the *refrains* of ballads always observe this rule and restore formal and musical interest thereby . . .

'What I have never understood if one reads by sense is what is the function of line-endings in syllabic verse? I sense a form, but only by attention to line-endings.'

In a later letter to me Mrs Daryush also deals with this last point: '. . . it seems often forgotten that mere permissiveness does not in itself make a new art form. It must be supported by other, counterpointing, disciplines, the more difficult because self-imposed. In syllabic verse, as I see it, the mere counting of syllables, though the only *actual* rule, is a very small part indeed of what is needed . . . Since power and style depend on the enhancing of sense and feeling by the form and emphasis of the metre, and since, perhaps, the most important emphasis is on the last word of the line, this becomes a sort of throne, often spotlighted by rhyme, and its occupant must be carefully chosen. Moreover, since in syllabic verse this emphasis is not indicated by stress-count, it has to be built up by a subtle internal accord of sense, feeling, grammar and music.'

I think there is in the lecture a partial answer to this in my remarks about end-stopping, but the thing is certainly somewhat mysterious. I asked Mrs Daryush in conversation whether she regarded rhyme as essential in syllabics. The sense of her reply was: not essential, but extremely helpful in getting over this very crux.

Finally, a phrase from one of Mrs Daryush's letters which strikingly sums matters up: 'In true syllabics there is no marching or dancing, only the natural dignity or grace of sincere and selfless purpose, whether of thought or mood.'

Both Pie and Custard

Writing to the editor of *The Dial* in 1922, Wallace Stevens said: 'Do please, excuse me from the biographical note. I am a lawyer and live in Hartford. But such facts are neither gay nor instructive.' However, the world has always found the facts enigmatic and fascinating. Even those never likely to read a line of Stevens have been keenly struck by the notion of one man combining the qualities that go to make an able lawyer and a poet not only of reputation but also of profundity and advanced style. During his lifetime Stevens's distaste for publicity made biographical facts and attitudes hard to come by, and after his death his letters were long anticipated in the expectation of their explaining the supposed incongruity between his two modes of existence, as artist and man of affairs. When the letters were published in 1967, what came out of them was the reverse of anything journalistically quirky or sensational in that department of Stevens's life: instead, the book drew a portrait sufficiently full and coherent to allay for ever the crude questionings, and one of far greater interest and subtlety than some no doubt imagined from the scanty lines previously available to view. It is true that the collection included nothing from the archives of the Hartford group of insurance companies which employed Stevens from 1916 until his death in 1955 and it may be expected that the biography which is being written by Samuel French Morse will interestingly and perhaps illuminatingly fill this gap. But enough details emerge from Stevens's private correspondence to fix, in true colours I would guess, the routine of his life as a lawyer, his relations with his stenographer, the companies' coloured chauffeurs, and other colleagues, and his own attitude to his professional work. As could have been deduced — for Stevens, far from trying to escape from the Hartford, went on working for them for five years beyond the compulsory retirement age — the tensions experienced by the poet were quite outside any mere clash of human types or division of time between office hours and art. The Hartford and their employees obviously held Stevens in respect and, when after a good many years, his poetic reputation became public property, pride: on his side there was no undue strain in his evolvement of a dignified and sometimes facetious affection, never false or condescending.

Critics have often said that Stevens's poetry is about poetry. Even when the critic is sympathetic I think there is always an implication of the pejorative in such a statement — a notion that thereby the poetry is unduly limited in scope or that the poet is a mere aesthete. I must say that it is a statement that it would have never occurred to me to make, but that is possibly because to me, too, poetry seems a legitimate, not at all an incestuous, theme for poetry. But anyway in Stevens's case the statement is misleading because of his very conception of 'poetry'. One of the most valuable pages of the *Letters* is the 'Memorandum' about a Chair of Poetry he sent to his friend Henry Church, a rich patron of the arts, director of the manufacturers of that commodity useful to poets, bicarbonate of soda, who had it in mind to found such a Chair at an American University. I want to quote two paragraphs from the Memorandum. They show, first, that for Stevens poetry was something more than metrical discourse, though one must add that his idea was far from the soppy one that conceives the 'poetic' and then includes within that term certain elevated prose, and certain phenomena, like sunsets or babies' smiles. The paragraphs also show how Stevens differed, in his view of poetry's supreme importance, from someone like Matthew Arnold who wanted it to govern conduct and belief in modern life: Stevens, it seems to me, in this latter area is at once more subtle and down to earth.

'What is intended', Stevens wrote to Henry Church, 'is to study the theory of poetry in relation to what poetry has been and in relation to what it ought to be. Its literature is a part of it, and only a part of it. For this purpose, poetry means not the language of poetry but the thing itself, wherever it may be found. It does not mean verse any more than philosophy means prose. The subject-matter of poetry is the thing to be ascertained. Off-hand the subject matter is what comes to mind when one says of the month of August . . .

"Thou art not August, unless I make thee so."
It is the aspects of the world and of men and women that have been added to them by poetry. These aspects are difficult to recognize and to measure.

'While aesthetic ideas are commonplaces in this field, its import is not the import of the superficial. The major poetic idea in the world is and always has been the idea of God. One of the visible movements of the modern imagination is the movement away from the idea of God. The poetry that created the idea of God will either adapt it to our different intelligence, or create a substitute for it, or make it unnecessary. These alternatives probably mean the same thing, but the intention is not to foster a cult. The knowledge of poetry is a part of philosophy, and a part of science; the import of poetry is the import of the spirit. The figures of the essential poets should be spiritual figures. The comedy of life or the tragedy of life as the material of an art, and the mold of life as the object of its creation are contemplated.'

Perhaps one doesn't take much away from these words at first reading or hearing — in his formal prose Stevens makes no more concessions to easy intelligibility than he does in his verse. But the ideas behind them are everywhere amplified in his work and I shall want to return to them later. Oddly enough, I think the most immediate phrase is that which he quotes from his poem called 'Asides on the Oboe' — 'Thou art not August, unless I make thee so.' For at the root of this, as we see at once, is the typically Stevensian notion that nature — the seasons, summer, August — is not real without human intervention, without the poetic power of giving to nature names and significant associations. But having said that, one must go on and make it absolutely clear that Stevens never ceased to be aware of nature's other reality — the brute, alien reality which is essentially inimical or at least indifferent to man. I know of no other poet who in his work was so constantly alive to what I would characterize as poetry's supreme task — to delineate the life of man in relation to nature unconsoled by any supernatural idea. So that if 'poetry' can be said to be the subject matter of all Stevens's poems, that subject matter is in fact all that makes a mysterious nature meaningful — or unmeaningful — to humankind.

I wonder whether it is too fanciful to suggest that Stevens's long lifetime of secular sensitivity to reality was sustained by his day to day absorption in business affairs. Certainly the relations between reality and poetry to be found everywhere in his work are paralleled by the relations of his office and his evening pursuits, and I don't think the analogy necessarily glib or superficial. Many artists are, through the very success of their art, led away from the tensions and the sources that brought it into being. And absorbed in the world of art they can become a prey to idealistic notions that their earlier years in the realer world would simply never have entertained. Spot illustrations are apt to be crude but the cases of D. H. Lawrence and T. S. Eliot spring to mind. It would be absurd to say that when the former left the Midlands, and the latter Lloyds Bank, decline set in, but it can hardly be denied that what is unsatisfactory in the later careers of both writers stems from a slackening of their hold on reality and the importation into their work of ideas that we can't help but feel to be false or at the least inappropriate.

*

At the time his daughter compiled the collection, nearly 3,300 of Stevens's letters were available for publication. Though not many more than a quarter were used and even from those some passages were omitted, the result is a very substantial volume of close on 900 pages. My feeling is that it is one of the great books of the twentieth century, to be ranked with other masterpieces in the same, almost accidental *genre* like Freud's letters to Wilhelm Fliess and Gide's *Journals,* a *genre* in which our times have so excelled. It is part of the book's extraordinary interest that right from its start it begins to delineate the twin themes of Stevens's life. He was born in 1879 and the earliest letters we have are a few he wrote to his mother from a summer camp at the age of fifteen. The syntax and vocabulary of these are already brilliant, but most significant is that they are full of close observation of people, objects and nature. The second letter in the book, amusingly prophetic, actually contains one of those verbal imitations of non-human sounds that were such a curious and persistent feature of his verse. In 1897 he went to Harvard, but only one letter has survived from his years there. In the *Letters* Miss Stevens has resourcefully filled the gap with extracts from a journal he began to keep in 1896 and with some letters from his father. The journal is full of observation, too, and of a Ruskinian precision: the letters from the father are quite remarkable.

Garrett Stevens was a successful though not wealthy lawyer in a country town in Pennsylvania. He had been born on a farm, had been a schoolteacher, and combined business and political interests with his attorney's practice. While Wallace was at Harvard the father, equally with the son, grasped the issues of the son's life that was to follow. The opposition between them was far from simply conventional. Certainly the father urged an orthodox career while the undergraduate son, like many undergraduate sons, vaguely contemplated a literary life; but Garrett Stevens had no doubt about the unusual nature of his son's talents. He wrote, quaintly but acutely: 'but for eccentricities in your genius you may be fitted for a Chair'. The son realized that the father was holding him, as he said, 'in check', but he had few

3*

illusions about his own character or the problems of material existence. He wrote in his journal: 'I am certainly a domestic creature, *par excellence*'; and 'I should be quite content to work and be practical — but I hate the conflict whether it "avails" or not. I want my powers to be put to their fullest use — to be exhausted when I am done with them. On the other hand I do not want to make a petty struggle for existence — physical or literary. I must try not to be dilettante — half dream, half deed. I must be all dream or all deed.' The extraordinary thing about Stevens's long life that lay ahead was not merely that it avoided the dilettante, that it was not (though superficially divided) 'half dream, half deed', but that of the alternatives proposed it is impossible to say in which it consisted. In a sense it was 'all dream' *and* 'all deed'. It was a fable of possible modern literary lives. It was aimed to disprove what his father had put to him in 1898 in so forcible, so quintessentially Stevensian a way: 'One never thinks out a destiny — If a fellow takes Peach Pie — he often wishes he had chosen the Custard . . . The only trouble is that since we cannot have *both* Pie and custard — it is oft too late to repent.'

After Harvard, Stevens worked as a journalist for a short period, neither successfully nor congenially. He had the notion of resigning from his newspaper and devoting himself to writing, but quite soon he fell in with his father's urging and took up the law. By 1904 he had passed his bar examinations and was admitted to practice. In the same year he met and fell in love with his future wife. Following his death she destroyed a number of his letters to her of this period (after first copying extracts she thought might be of interest), but this is probably no great loss. The letters of the long courtship that remain are curiously pointless, a parallel to Stevens's career as a lawyer — and, indeed, as a writer — during the same epoch. He started a law firm but it was a failure. He then worked in several law practices without apparently making any mark. Lone wolf business skill, the flair for acquiring clients, are not qualities possessed by shy men, and Stevens was certainly shy. He was big and, judging by his

photographs, at all stages of his life handsome, but the formida-
bility noted by many arose probably quite unconsciously out of
his brain-power, lack of ease in direct personal contacts and, no
doubt, his occasional exasperation at other men's disorder and
importunity (what he characterized as his 'pretty well-developed
mean streak'). Besides, with age and distinction shyness often
becomes something mysteriously other in the eyes of the outside
world. Stevens's sexual desires were from the outset directed
towards uxoriousness. And the *fin de siècle* literary tradition his
adolescence inevitably inherited persisted with him for a very
long time: as late as 1907 he was quoting Andrew Lang's Odyssey
sonnet with approval.

But in 1908 he was freed from the antipathies of private
practice by becoming employed as a lawyer by an insurance
company. The following year he was earning enough to be able
to marry. His father died in 1911 and his mother a year later. A
sentence from his journal about his dying mother is one of the
few indications in his letters and journal of this time of his future
literary power: 'the beating of her heart in the veins of her throat
was as rapid as water running from a bottle'. It is quite out of the
blue, so far as the reader of the correspondence is concerned,
that the letters appear to the editor of the magazine, *Poetry*. The
first, another laconic response to a request for a biographical
note, is dated November 6, 1914: the second, which follows
without intervening material, is dated June 6, 1915, and discusses
the order of the sections of what has developed into Stevens's
most celebrated poem, 'Sunday Morning'. Somehow he had
become a modern poet.

I feel sure that, as I've suggested, the changes in his personal
life played a part in his being enabled to write the extraordinary
early poems of his first book, *Harmonium*. The bases of his
existence had hardened through marriage, and through employment which gave scope to his desire for a place in the world while
removing the drawbacks to that desire inherent in the poetic
character. The death of parents is, too, not only a time of emotion
and past emotion recollected: it also often prefigures, in a strange

but not inexplicable way, a deeper achievement in the child. On the purely literary side we can see now that in the poems of *Harmonium* Stevens was liberated from explicit meaning, from the commonplaces of the tradition of his youth, through his reading of the French symbolists, a process similar to that undergone by T. S. Eliot. A large part of his initial power resides in his extraordinary gift for iambic verse, his feeling for and interest in vocabulary, which freed from the compulsion to narrate in any prose sense flourish in startling, evocative, exotic and disturbing style:

> *The man in Georgia waking among pines*
> *Should be pine-spokesman. The responsive man,*
> *Planting his pristine cores in Florida,*
> *Should prick thereof, not on the psaltery,*
> *But on the banjo's categorical gut,*
> *Tuck, tuck, while the flamingo flapped his bays.*
> *Sepulchral señors, bibbling pale mescal,*
> *Oblivious to the Aztec almanacs,*
> *Should make the intricate Sierra scan.*
> *And dark Brazilians in their cafés,*
> *Musing immaculate, pampean dits,*
> *Should scrawl a vigilant anthology,*
> *To be their latest, lucent paramour.*

Later in life he was quite patient with correspondents who asked him to 'explain' passages in his poetry, particularly the famous pieces in *Harmonium* like 'The Comedian as the Letter C' from which I've just quoted. His further inexplicitness is often amusing. Though a good deal of Stevens is not really as difficult as was once — as, indeed, is often still — thought, the 'nonsense' side of the modern movement in verse — the arbitrary symbols, the private references, the unexplained personae and fragmentary plots — persisted with him, in fact, until the end. (It accounts for a large part of that growth sector of the American literary economy, the Stevens critical industry, only rivalled perhaps by Dylan Thomas Exegesis Unlimited.) But, of course, if this were all there were to him he would merely share a place with a score of others. As it is, the conviction grows that he must be placed with the two or three greatest English-speaking poets of the twentieth century.

This sense is uncontradicted by the *Letters*, though the epochs they mainly record are unsensational indeed. Stevens moved to Hartford, Connecticut, in 1916, having followed a former associate to join the Hartford group of insurance companies. His early years with them involved a fair amount of travel, including trips to Florida, which subsequently became a favourite vacation place, and this experience gave concreteness to the Americanness of his verse and in particular established the important polarity of rigorous New England and the lush tropics. He observed flora and fauna (in gardens and zoos as well as at large) with the old Ruskinian intensity. The first edition of *Harmonium* was published in 1923 and the following year his first and only child was born (about the possibility of a second child he characteristically said later: 'There is nothing I should have liked more, but I was afraid of it.') Between that time and the second, enlarged edition of *Harmonium* in 1931 he clearly worked harder at law than at poetry. But once again a more settled background, the opportunity to become more comfortably 'a domestic creature', provided the conditions for a renewal of creativity. In 1932 he bought the spacious house he was to live in for the rest of his life — previously he had been a tenant in far from luxurious conditions. Soon after, he was established in an impregnable position with his insurance company, his travelling on business infrequent. From this time the typed letter became the rule rather than the exception as his office status enabled him to use his stenographer to dictate his private correspondence, and a characteristic tone of voice emerged.

Then followed the greater part of his correspondence, as we have it, and absorbing it is, even heroic. He sustained with a succession of correspondents an intercourse sometimes ironic, often subtly affectionate, always astonishingly polished and intelligent. Even what came to be the immutable routines of his existence are made continually fresh. It is no exaggeration to say that the material foundation of the great bulk of his verse is his observation of nature as it existed between his office and his house, in his garden and in the nearby park. The scene never became commonplace or taken for granted through familiarity. The observation of seasons, sky, trees and birds is perpetually fresh. But the miracle is that such observation is usually merely a point of departure for constantly rich and unexpected verbal, philosophical and fictional fantasias. I'd like to read a poem called 'Of Hartford in a Purple Light' from what may be called Stevens's middle period, to show this transfiguring power. It is by no means one of his finest poems, but it stands conveniently between the extravagances of his first period and the rather soberer naturalism of his last. Perhaps only poets who have wrestled to get on paper the significance in their minds of ordinary objects will fully appreciate the achievement here, but imagine trying to transfigure Lichfield or Halifax in twenty-seven lines.

A long time you have been making the trip
From Havre to Hartford, Master Soleil,
Bringing the lights of Norway and all that.

A long time the ocean has come with you,
Shaking the water off, like a poodle,
That splatters incessant thousands of drops,

Each drop a petty tricolor. For this,
The aunts in Pasadena, remembering,
Abhor the plaster of the western horses,

Souvenirs of museums. But, Master, there are
Lights masculine and lights feminine.
What is this purple, this parasol,

This stage-light of the Opera?
It is like a region full of intonings.
It is Hartford seen in a purple light.

A moment ago, light masculine,
Working, with big hands, on the town,
Arranged its heroic attitudes.

But now as in an amour of women
Purple sets purple round. Look, Master,
See the river, the railroad, the cathedral . . .

When male light fell on the naked back
Of the town, the river, the railroad were clear.
Now, every muscle slops away.

Hi! Whisk it, poodle, flick the spray
Of the ocean, ever-freshening,
On the irised hunks, the stone bouquet.

Only in the last few years of his life did Stevens seem to find arduous this burden of day to day office work, the morning and evening and weekend poetic response. He wrote in his seventieth year: 'I begin to feel at the end of the day that I am through for that day. It is not that I grow tired but that my elan seems somewhat bent. I should much rather stroll home looking at the girls than anything else.' Also remarkable was his continued alertness to art, to new poets and periodicals and correspondents; and I would certainly connect this with the necessity, in prolonging his life as an active lawyer, of keeping up to date in that department too. 'I have never been bored in any general sense,' he once observed, and on the evidence of the *Letters* we can unhesitatingly believe him. I wouldn't want to leave this aspect of Stevens without saying that he himself was perfectly aware of the objections to his existence as the existence of a poet which many of you have no doubt been silently raising. Mentioning his forthcoming collection of poems, *Auroras of Autumn*, in a letter of 1949 he said: 'I don't know how the book will be regarded', adding: 'It is not easy to experience much in the rather routine life that I lead. While one is never sure that it makes much difference, one is equally never sure that it doesn't.'

Of course, Stevens was not speaking here of his avoidance of a superficial Bohemianism (if that adjective is ever really needed to qualify that substantive). There is a passage in one of his letters of 1935 which encapsulates his attitude on this question. At that time his books were first issued in limited editions by the Alcestis Press which for one of them used a designer and printer called Lew Ney. Mr Ney had picked up the corrected proofs of the book from Stevens in Hartford. Stevens, in a letter to the owner of the press which does not appear in the published correspondence, had apparently made some remarks critical of the printer. The following passage appears in a further letter from Stevens to the owner of the press: 'My sole purpose in dropping you this note is to make quite sure that nothing I have said about Mr Ney will affect your relations with him. Confidentially, he suggested that he and his wife would be touring this part of the world on foot and *in shorts* before long, and promised to call on me. The office here is a solemn affair of granite, with a portico resting on five of the grimmest columns. The idea of Mr Ney and his wife toddling up the front steps and asking for me made me suggest that they might like to stop at some nearby rest-house and change to something more bourgeois. This is merely one of the hilarious possibilities of being in the insurance business. After all, why should one worry?' The words 'in shorts' are underlined by Stevens: offhand, the only example of underlining one recalls in the whole of the correspondence.

One advantage of his life that cannot be gainsaid was his being able largely to avoid literary chores like reviewing and public readings, which add nothing to a writer's essential impact and, by wasting his time and lulling him into a false sense of achievement, positively detract from what he may have to offer. The monetary motive for such activities was absent but Stevens was also strong-minded about them. Though here again one feels that Stevens's assured position in his other world may have been a reason for his uninterest in keeping his name before the public through literary journalism and suchlike, as it probably was in his rewarding patience before publishing his first book and, later, his *Collected Poems*. Certainly the copiousness of his verse shows that given a reasonable life span a poet's other job need not disqualify him from major status.

Quite late in his life his growing eminence compelled him to respond to a number of invitations to lecture and contribute essays, for occasions usually of inescapable distinction. Most of the pieces that resulted are reprinted in his prose book, *The Necessary Angel*. They are not easy going, but I think that the reader who gradually gets to know the poetry will want to dip into them — and will emerge with greater understanding. It would be beyond the scope of this lecture to try to give an adequate account of Stevens's ideas about poetry. Luckily, what I would have liked to do in this field has already been done. As I've said, there's already a dismaying quantity of literature about Stevens but among it the little book by Frank Kermode in the 'Writers and Critics' series seems to me outstandingly excellent and useful as to both the poetry and the ideas. On this occasion I want to take up just one point relevant to my theme. In *The Necessary Angel* Stevens, in the form of a question, raises the 'possibility that poetry is only reality, after all, and that poetic truth is factual truth, seen, it may be, by those whose range in the perception of fact — that is, whose sensibility — is greater than our own'.

This equating of poetry with reality, however tentative, I find very moving. There is nothing ill-considered or sentimental about it. The essay in which it appears begins, in fact, with some remarks and quotations designed to explode the notion that any human ideas can transcend the problems offered by the confrontation of the material universe, notably part of a letter from the philosopher, Henry Bradley, to Robert Bridges, as follows: 'My own attitude towards all philosophies old or new, is very sceptical. Not that I despise philosophy or philosophers; but I feel that the universe of being is too vast to be comprehended even by the greatest of the sons of Adam. We do get, I believe, glimpses of the real problems, perhaps even of the real solutions; but when we have formulated our questions, I fear we have always substituted illusory problems for the real ones.' If, Stevens says in this same essay, philosophic truth may be said to be the official view of being, he would define poetry 'as an unofficial view of being'.

The essential alienation of man from the universe is a constant theme of Stevens's own verse, nowhere expressed with more clarity and poignancy than in the later 'Notes Toward a Supreme Fiction', which Kermode, I think rightly, calls his greatest poem. But for Stevens the alienation is the source, not the daunting, of poetic creativity:

> *From this the poem springs: that we live in a place*
> *That is not our own and, much more, not ourselves*
> *And hard it is in spite of blazoned days.*
>
> *We are the mimics. Clouds are pedagogues*
> *The air is not a mirror but bare board,*
> *Coulisse bright-dark, tragic chiaroscuro*
>
> *And comic colour of the rose, in which*
> *Abyssmal instruments make sounds like pips*
> *Of the sweeping meanings that we add to them.*

As Stevens says later in the poem, the task is 'not to console/ Nor sanctify, but plainly to propound.' It follows from all this, I think, that the long series of Stevens's poems is constantly sustained by the conviction that poetry's apprehension of reality alone gives meaning to existence, while the poetry is saved from aestheticism or from anything else smacking of the high falutin by a sombre and indeed pessimistic sense of the terrible and un-caring realities behind the skies and trees observed by the poet with so much accuracy and love. The great triumph of the 'Notes Toward a Supreme Fiction' is that when at the high point of the poem Stevens introduces an apparently transcendental notion — an angel — we feel not just that the splendour of the verse has earned such a symbol but that the poet is still dealing with reality, that he is still fundamentally neither consoling nor sanctifying. This is a sense we do not always get from poetry similarly — and marvellously — elevated, Rilke's *Duino Elegies*. There is absolutely no trace in Stevens — and we can't, I feel, always say this about Rilke — of play-acting, of unjustified assumptions made. The angel is a necessary one.

What am I to believe? If the angel in his cloud,
Serenely gazing at the violent abyss,
Plucks on his strings to pluck abysmal glory,

Leaps downward through evening's revelations, and
On his spredden wings, needs nothing but deep space,
Forgets the gold centre, the golden destiny,

Grows warm in the motionless motion of his flight,
Am I that imagine this angel less satisfied?
Are the wings his, the lapis-haunted air?

Is it he or is it I that experience this?
Is it I then that keep saying there is an hour
Filled with expressible bliss, in which I have

No need, am happy, forget need's golden hand,
Am satisfied without solacing majesty,
And if there is an hour there is a day,

There is a month, a year, there is a time
In which majesty is a mirror of the self:
I have not but I am and as I am, I am.

These external regions, what do we fill them with
Except reflections, the escapades of death,
Cinderella fulfilling herself beneath the roof?

In the *Letters* the question of poetry and reality is a constant preoccupation and the remarks here are all the more stimulating for the informality of their setting. They are a mine, I would think, for young poets. I want to quote just two of them. After he returned the proofs of the Faber *Selected Poems* in 1952, Stevens said: 'The book seemed rather slight and small to me — and unbelievably irrelevant to our actual world. It may be that all poetry has seemed like that at all times and always will. The close approach to reality has always been the supreme difficulty of any art: the communication of actuality as [poetics?] has been not only impossible, but has never appeared to be worth while because it loses identity as the event passes. Nothing in the world is deader than yesterday's political (or realistic) poetry. Nevertheless the desire to combine the two things, poetry and reality, is a constant desire.' This is the other quotation, from a letter of 1949: 'The demand for reality in poetry brings one sooner or later to a point where it becomes almost impossible since a real poetry, that is to say, a poetry that is not poetical or that is not merely the notation of objects in themselves poetic is a poetry divested of poetry. That is what I am trying to get at the moment. Perhaps I am not young enough for it, or old enough ... The bare idea makes everything else seem false and verbose and even ugly.'

Almost from the outset Stevens was seen to be a great master of language: increasingly he is being recognized as a poet of organic development and Rilkean penetration who had things to say about the human condition of our time of extreme importance. However, my sense is that despite such discrimination as shown in Kermode's in several ways pioneering book his later work is still undervalued. The easiest way into Stevens — and no one can pretend that he is an easily approachable poet — is possibly through the final poems, where he is after 'the bare idea', 'the poetry divested of poetry'. In these we have the old accurate observation of nature and the seasons but largely unaccompanied by the old fictions and fantasies:

> Silence is a shape that has passed.
> Otu-bre's lion-roses have turned to paper
> And the shadows of the trees
> Are like wrecked umbrellas.
>
> The effete vocabulary of summer
> No longer says anything.

The brown at the bottom of red
The orange far down in yellow,

Are falsifications from a sun
In a mirror, without heat,
In a constant secondariness,
A turning down toward finality —

Except that a green plant glares, as you look
At the legend of the maroon and olive forest,
Glares, outside of the legend, with the barbarous green
Of the harsh reality of which it is part.

The correspondence reveals sparse English interest in Stevens's work. There is, for instance, an appreciative letter of 1938 on being noticed in Julian Symons's little magazine, *Twentieth Century Verse*; some abortive negotiations as to possible publication with the Fortune Press; a comment on a review of *Ideas of Order* in *New Verse*, a review headed 'Stuffed Goldfinch', quite notorious at the time. About this last, Stevens mildly remarked to his correspondent: 'What you say about the Pulitzer Prize is interesting. After all, there are people who think that IDEAS OF ORDER is not only bad but rotten' — a remark all the more ironical because it can be seen to occur in a truly distinguished series of letters about poetry to the proprietor of the Alcestis Press. Typical of Stevens is that even after this review he was recommending *New Verse* as 'the best poetry magazine', and its editor, the author of the review, as one with 'his eye on the right values'. Of course, with all Stevens's later development before us, we cannot begin to understand how the book that Stevens's more ribald legal friends called *Ordeals of Ida* seemed to Geoffrey Grigson finicky, rhythmless, unreal, inhuman and to observe nothing. And one would guess that even after the delayed accolade of the Faber imprint of 1952, Stevens's English admirers have not been numerous. By an ill chance even the publication of his *Collected Poems* was posthumous here. It had been published in America to coincide with his seventy-fifth birthday on October

2, 1954. Just over six months later he underwent an operation that showed he was suffering from an inevitably fatal cancer. The fact was kept from him and he made a sufficient recovery from the surgery to go to Yale to receive an honorary degree and actually to return, at the end of June and into July, to his office at the Hartford for a few hours a day. Only a phrase from his last published letter, dated July 15, 1955, reveals any real relaxing of his hold on the two preoccupations of his life — 'Considering my present condition I can neither concentrate on poetry nor enjoy poetry.' These are harrowing words, following the long years of asserting, in so many different ways, poetry to be life's only sanction, and of striving so elaborately to show in his art the nature of human existence; and one recalls his apothegm in his collection of such items, *Adagia* — 'Poetry is a health'. But the phrase of renunciation comes, after all, in a brief note written to try to help a young poet quite unknown to him. By August 2 he was dead.

POSTSCRIPT

Some of the material in the foregoing lecture came from a review I wrote of *The Letters of Wallace Stevens* for *The Times Literary Supplement*. The reference in the review to the *New Verse* notice drew a letter from Geoffrey Grigson which it is only fair — as well as interesting — to reprint here:

'It is curious to be faced, all of a sudden, with an exhumed judgement of one's early days. *The Stuffed Goldfinch* . . . I had forgotten this heading to a review of Wallace Stevens's *Ideas of Order* written thirty-one years ago; and now have had to observe your reviewer of *The Letters of Wallace Stevens* putting myself of that time on corrective exhibition. So I looked up the review, which I am assured is "notorious", and I wondered — if I was not right.

'Certain charges against the verse of Wallace Stevens were made in a very few sentences; and having gone back since 1936, at intervals, when the cry of greatness, greatness has resounded (usually in the academic echo-chamber) to try Wallace Stevens again, I would still think this poet of unvarying taste a "single artificer of his own world of mannerism", who substituted coldly for the heart's sunshine "an uneasy subjective twinkle of sequins", "describing thirteen ways of seeing a blackbird, forgetting the bird".

' "Wise after the event," says your reviewer. After what *event*? A consensus in the English departments of universities that Wallace's non-poetry on ice, charming in so many ways except the one which would remove the negative, is to be adulated? "How pathetic is the sparse evidence . . . of English interest in his work." This is the tone, I think, of the superior bully — what if the unimpressed English were right, including the one who could not feel a heart in the stuffing of the goldfinch, charming bird, mounted no doubt on a dry thistle, in a cultural, instead of a natural history tableau, in a facsimile museum? Great master of language? Yes, but in poems? He observes, he observes, says your reviewer, once slipping in the dubious compliment "Ruskinian", — and I would repeat that he describes his thirteen ways of seeing the blackbird, without the bird. Applying to Stevens his dictum that "poetry has to do with reality in its most individual aspect", I would reiterate that with him, no dishonourable forger, the individual aspect is his own, not reality's, with a string of frigid consequences.

'If I accuse critics of exalting a sterile, germless, nerveless, unreverberant imagism, it is not to have a smack at this honourable poet. It is because excessive praise for the verse of Wallace Stevens is among the conditions which now encourage so much verse without the charm of his virtues, but with an assortment of his vices. What might do good is less extension of an English critical begging-bowl to some American values, less pragmatic analysis (reminding me of a staircase exhibit at the Fogg of everything, pigment, medium, ground, etc, which constitutes a renaissance picture) and a little more Geneva criticism, minus the metaphysics; a little more respect for Whitman, and for roll, rise, carol, and creation. Or one might think hard about Wallace Stevens between transmuted realities represented, let us say, by Alexander Pope and, in another art, by the exquisite submission to reality of a Ben Nicholson.'

My printed reply to this letter was simply to say that 'wise after the event' was an incompletely explained phrase I was conscious of after passing the proof — 'hindsight' would have been better in the context — but that the event I meant to imply was, of course, *Ideas of Order* as a prelude to the bigger proportion of Stevens's work and not as a mere addendum to *Harmonium*. My lecture makes this clear.

V

The Filthy Aunt
and the Anonymous Seabird

A poem I wish I had never written concerns the finding by the poet of a spider in the bath. Though far from successful it has been a good deal anthologized, no doubt because constituting one of the few occasions when I have reflected archetypal experience. I quote the second of its five stanzas:

Next day with some surprise one finds it there.
It seems to have moved an inch or two, perhaps.
It starts to take on that familiar air
Of prisoners for whom time is erratic:
The filthy aunt forgotten in the attic.

In an anthology edited by a Doctor of Philosophy of this university, himself a considerable poet, the last line I have quoted — 'The filthy aunt forgotten in the attic' — has the following note: 'a painting, of course'. He intended to be helpful, bless his heart, but he was wrong. I meant a literal aunt, literally filthy, and, quite apart from any force and humour the poem might be thought to have, this reading is surely required because of the reference to prisoners in the previous line.

I'm not sure where our editor's note should be placed in the categories of misreadings of a poem enumerated in I. A. Richards's *Practical Criticism*. 'Stock response'? 'Arbitrary rendering'? 'Moral objection'? Even, possibly, 'anti-religious reaction'. But it's not my purpose this afternoon to look at the meaning of poetry with Richards's intellectual rigour and ordering power, even if I were capable of doing so. I want rather to consider the question from the poet's point of view — what minimum understanding he asks from his reader and, *per contra*, what his obligations may be to remove possibilities of misunderstanding.

I suppose for the poet meaning is like beauty and the audience for his poem — his eye is simply not on those particular balls. I cannot imagine any decent poet setting out to write 'beautiful' verse. No doubt at certain stages of composition, perhaps particularly in second and subsequent drafts, he may exercise a choice in favour of procedures hallowed by critical tradition as likely to result in memorability, authority — beauty. He may, for instance, call in 'apt alliteration's artful aid' where the choice of an epithet is still in balance. And the process when at certain moments the poet feels that a poem takes off — moments of inspiration not entirely volitional — such process is to a degree determined, I don't question, by his tradition, his knowledge (not always conscious) of what has worked in the poetry of the past. But the poet's overwhelming sense is that if he gets his conception down beauty will take care of itself. So, too, I'm sceptical whether a poet ever has an audience in mind during the process of composition. Even in epochs like our own, when his audience has been measured in hundreds, the poet writes, as Wordsworth said, for men.

Getting 'his conception down'. Into this operation, of course, the element of meaning enters, but for the poet it is a very different element than for the reader. For the poet the success of the operation is not directly related to clarity of expression. Indeed, the very business of carrying a poem through a number of drafts may take the poem's text farther and farther from its primal meaning. Consider the first two lines of Yeats's 'Under Ben Bulben':

Swear by what the sages spoke
Round the Mareotic Lake . . .

And now Yeats's very first draft of the poem:

I believe what the old saints
a thousand years before Christ, sitting under
the palms, like the old saints about
the Mareotic sea . . .

For the critic, too — the self-appointed mediator between the poet and the reader — meaning is not the same as meaning for the poet. One is full of admiration, for example, for William Empson's delination of ambiguity in poetry — and what he has said must certainly have had some effect on the practice of poets since 1930 — but the pleasures and puzzles of ambiguity are not deliberately written into poetry. One boggles even more at the ineffable exegesis in the ideological sphere of other critics, mainly American. However, the examples I'm going to give have not been chosen for comic effect and one at least comes from a book of not negligible insight. The passages in question deal with four lines in the opening sonnet of Dylan Thomas's 'Altarwise by owl-light' sequence. Here is the beginning of the sonnet:

Altarwise by owl-light in the half-way house
The gentleman lay graveward with his furies;
Abaddon in the hangnail cracked from Adam,
And, from his fork, a dog among the fairies,
The atlas-eater with a jaw for news,
Bit out the mandrake with to-morrow's scream.

Elder Olson, in his book *The Poetry of Dylan Thomas*, takes the protagonist here to be Hercules, deriving this from the constellation Hercules which declines to the west after the autumnal equinox, the 'half-way house'. Hercules, says Olson, 'is mortal, possesses like the rest of us, destruction and perdition implicit in the flesh derived from Adam. A "dog among the fairies", Cerberus, the symbol of death, with its three heads which can smell out the seed and devour all, a head for each age of man, bites out the seed of his loins. Cerberus is a dog, and the only real thing, for Thomas, among the pagan myths; death is the solid fact amid all our fancies. He guards the Equator; he watches the regions of Tartarus, that is, the realms of death. Death will at last devour the world; hence he is "the atlas-eater". He has "a jaw for news" because he can smell out the seed. In such a world, ruled by death, to-morrow can bring only horror; hence he bites out "the mandrake" from the fork or loin. The astronomical phenomenon behind all this is that as Canis Major, the Greater Dog, rises, the constellation Hercules and the head of Draco set. Hercules is represented . . . with one foot upon Draco; thus we have the mandrake (man-dragon, and "drake" is the old word for dragon) bitten out from his fork by the dog. Since the mandrake was thought to shriek on being pulled out, and since it is the seed that has been devoured, we have "to-morrow's scream".'

H. H. Kleinman devoted a whole book to these sonnets: he called it *The Religious Sonnets of Dylan Thomas*. Hercules makes no appearance in his explication of the passage. As he says, 'The identity of the gentleman "in the half-way house" is unknown to us. Is he God about to descend to mortality ("graveward")? Or is the gentleman Abaddon? Or is he Christ? He is all three in one: he is God, he is Christ, he is Abaddon.' I pass over two pages of exegesis, and continue the quotation: 'The presence of Abaddon "in the hang-nail cracked from Adam" reminds us of mortality brought into the world through Adam's sin. But Abaddon is not the only descendant of Adam; Christ, too, in the flesh, is kin to Adam. (In Luke 3:23–38 Christ's genealogy is traced to Adam.) The hangnail image is a typical Thomas pun: a hangnail, literally, is a cracked piece of skin hanging from the finger. As a metaphor, "hangnail" contains genealogy and prophecy: it is a statement that Christ (the cuticle) is descended from Adam (the finger), and it is a prediction that Christ will hang nailed to the Cross.' Then follows an account of the mandrake legend and Thomas's particular use of it. The journalistic metaphor in the lines is next discussed and Kleinman arrives at the word 'fairies'. 'The "fairies" among whom the dog bites out the mandrake are puzzling creatures. Are they the sexless angels of Abaddon's retinue? Are they the creatures abroad this magic night who are charged with announcing an important event? Are they in opposition to the furies? Are they the furies transformed into a half-rhyme by the poet as conjuror? Perhaps the furies and fairies are an echo of Marcellus' description of the time of Christ's nativity . . . The dog may be Christ, the hound of heaven, who bites out the mandrake (man) from the fork or loins of Abaddon, thus redeeming man from sin (Adam) and death (Abaddon). "Tomorrow's scream" foretells the Crucifixion at the same time that it suggests screaming headlines of the event.' A further page of commentary on the lines follows.

In such an indiscriminate spattering of the target a few bulls can scarcely fail to be registered. But my feeling is that for the critic — and for his solemn readers — the poem has disappeared in favour of some sacred text whose sense, purpose and value — assuming it to have had them — have been lost sight of, perhaps for ever. How far, even in such extravagantly symbolist verse as early Thomas, does such exhaustive attempted interpretation have a part to play?

The lines 'The atlas-eater with a jaw for news / Bit out the mandrake with to-morrow's scream' were the subject of a pioneer interpretation by a reviewer of the book in which they appeared, Edith Sitwell. She said that they referred to 'the violent speed and the sensation-loving, horror-loving craze of modern life'. Dylan Thomas's own comment on this analysis was that it seemed to him 'a bit vague'. He added: 'She doesn't take the literal meaning: that a world-devouring ghost-creature bit out the horror of to-morrow from a gentleman's loins.' Though Thomas went on with a few sentences of paraphrase, we must surely feel that he was right to insist on the primacy of the text, for if that is not right, nothing is. Undoubtedly the poet will require his reader to know who Abaddon was and to have some familiarity with the mandrake legend, but from then on, so far as he is concerned, the lines are on their own.

I want to turn now to a poem less obscure than the Dylan Thomas sonnet, Poem XXIX in W. H. Auden's 1930 *Poems* which appears in a truncated form in the *Collected Shorter Poems* under the title 'Consider'. An analysis of this poem forms part of what is on the whole a case against Auden in A. Alvarez's book *The Shaping Spirit*. The book dates from 1958 and probably Alvarez would not now put his case in the same way: certainly I am not resuscitating what I think to be a lapse of critical judgment with malice aforethought — the story happens to end with a twist against myself.

Auden's poem begins with a bird's eye or airman's view of bourgeois life — of the garden party and the luxury hotel. Then, in the second paragraph, the poet addresses the personification of some force or principle in history or life, a personification he calls 'supreme Antagonist'.

> *Long ago, supreme Antagonist,*
> *More powerful than the great northern whale*
> *Ancient and sorry at life's limiting defect,*
> *In Cornwall, Mendip, or the Pennine moor*
> *Your comments on the highborn mining-captains,*
> *Found they no answer, made them wish to die*
> *— Lie since in barrows out of harm.*
> *You talk to your admirers every day*
> *By silted harbours, derelict works,*
> *In strangled orchards, and the silent comb*
> *Where dogs have worried or a bird was shot . . .*

I don't think Alvarez's five or so pages of explication get near any plausible view of the meaning of the poem as a whole. And on the part of the poem whose start I've quoted he says: 'in the second section of the poem an enormous machinery of Fate is rumbled into motion, with full Anglo-Saxon trappings and an obscure mythology to go with it (that "great northern whale", for example; if he is immortal, then he can't be an ordinary whale; whilst Moby Dick, my only other candidate, had his hunting grounds mostly in the southern hemisphere). The aim seems to

be to create a sort of modern epic, complete with a modern hero—
"the hawk . . . or the helmeted airman"—in which heroic
action and Fate will combine to purge society.' And later Alvarez
adds: 'What the dissatisfied, the warped and the diseased have to
do with the purgation of society is by no means clear' — and 'I
am hard put to [sic] know what the poem is at.'

In Alvarez's irrelevant speculations about the whale we may
see evidence of the free association method of American academic
criticism, used here without sympathy for its subject, however,
unlike the case of the Dylan Thomas sonnet. But Alvarez's
more general bafflement before what, after all, is a poem that has
made its mark on several generations of readers must leave poets
with a sense of unease about the fate of their own even less
critically considered work.

When I reviewed Alvarez's book in *The London Magazine*
soon after it appeared I said complacently that 'One had always
thought that this brilliant and celebrated poem was about the
threat of death — the poem's "supreme Antagonist"— to various
characterized members of modern society and to that society
itself.' I was suitably chastened when I read recently, in *A Reader's
Guide to W. H. Auden*, the following: 'Critics take the "supreme
Antagonist" to be death, but the tautology implicit in death
making the highborn mining-captains "wish to die" seems clumsy.
Both the Old English *Bestiary* and *Paradise Lost* (1,200) compare
the whale with Satan, as, I believe, Auden is doing. In Auden's
glossary of Christian and psychological terms (BM Notebook,
fol. 44) Satan is seen as the Censor, responsible for repressing
man's natural instincts and bringing about that self-consciousness
which separates him from the rest of the animal kingdom. It is
this division in men and society, keeping them from their real
desires, that Auden is anatomizing in the poem. The Antagonist's
admirers, the ill, are in ascendancy and are themselves responsible
for the malaise, the "immeasurable neurotic dread", which
conditions them.' This is a view which seems undoubtedly
correct.

My great predecessor in this Chair, A. C. Bradley, once

excellently put the position about the poem and the critical commentary. I am indebted to a forthcoming book by Catherine Cooke for this passage from a letter from Bradley to Gilbert Murray. 'Perhaps', Bradley wrote, 'most people who are more or less fond of poetry do not *want* to do what I should call reading and understanding the poem — i.e. making the same process occur in themselves as occurred in the poet's head — but rather want what may be called the effect of the poem — i.e. something vaguer which is produced in them by reading the words. And if this is so I understand why commentaries annoy them so much. Perhaps too they are right so far as this, that there may be more imaginative activity in the vague process which the poem sets up in them than they would exert in the attempt to re-create the poet's process. I mean that it is hard to imagine as the poet did without losing something of the more general effect that one gets from one's first reading in which lots of detail is really not reproduced at all.'

I think that what Bradley says here reinforces my notion that exhaustive commentary is self-defeating — that, say, anyone who read Kleinman before reading Dylan Thomas's so-called 'Religious Sonnets' would perhaps never receive from them the poetic effect intended by the poet, the effect of warning, startling, instructing, his contemporaries. Commentary of its nature tends to be self-proliferating: its limits set not by the poet's purpose but the industry and ingenuity of the commentator. There was a trivial but significant example in a recent book of commentary on Yeats. The reference to the painter Calvert in 'Under Ben Bulben' is beyond a doubt a reference to the Calvert who was a disciple of William Blake and the friend of Samuel Palmer. But the commentator, having done his homework, could not resist casting his note in this form: 'Calvert: Denis Calvert (Calvaert) 1540–1619 was a Flemish painter who founded the School of Bologna and was the master of Guido Reni; but Yeats is here probably thinking of Edward Calvert (1799–1883) an English visionary artist on whom he once thought of writing a book.' One wonders if some wretched research graduate won't some day go looking at Denis Calvert's paintings to try to find in them something apposite to the poem. In any case, Yeats's line is for ever just that bit blurred.

It is also true that the 'general effect' of Auden's 'Consider' communicated itself at once to his sympathetic readers in the context of 1930, long before they were instructed about his High Church bias, his distortion of Marxism, his interest in Groddeck, Old English and mining engineering, his youth in the Midlands. On the other hand, once a poem ceases to be contemporary in that sense — and the period for this obviously varies with the nature of the poem — some imaginative historical placing must be done by the reader.

In the long run, I suppose, the poet would consider it vital for the reader to comprehend completely his central theme; he would also like, but not think it essential, for his external references to be picked up. What might be called the poem's *internal* references — its logic, its prosodic effects, its connections back and forth — the poet would be confident that some readers some day would tumble to them. In all this the professional reader — the critic — can obviously be of help: indeed, under modern academic conditions the help is inescapable. I would like to suggest that the model for it should be a book like Bradley's own *Commentary on Tennyson's In Memoriam* published in 1901. Bradley's procedure, after his long general introduction, is to deal with the poem section by section, prefacing his notes to each section with a usually brief outline of the section's theme. Where the section is puzzling or ambiguous Bradley's thematic exposition is correspondingly ample, but he takes a view, always a sensible and considered one, though leaving grounds for disagreement, if disagreement is possible. His notes are as short as is consonant with providing the fullest help: external references, literary and factual, are given, and there are cross-references to other parts of the poem. There is an occasional and most judicious assessment of aesthetic merit or demerit. The book is perhaps little known now so I may be forgiven if I show how it deals with the three-stanza section XXXIX.

Old warder of these buried bones,
  And answering now my random stroke
  With fruitful cloud and living smoke,
Dark yew, that graspest at the stones

And dippest toward the dreamless head,
  To thee too comes the golden hour
  When flower is feeling after flower;
But Sorrow — fixt upon the dead,

And darkening the dark graves of men,—
  What whispered from her lying lips?
  Thy gloom is kindled at the tips,
And passes into gloom again.

Bradley's general exposition refers to sections II and III of the
poem, from which come the phrases 'graspest at the stones', 'the
dreamless head', and 'lying lips'. In section II the yew tree was
said to preserve an unchanging gloom. In the present section the
poet acknowledges that this was a falsehood of Sorrow's; for
in Spring the gloom of the yew is 'kindled at the tips'. ' "Yes,"
answers Sorrow, "but it passes back into gloom." ' In his notes
Bradley explains the lines 'And answering now my random stroke/
With fruitful cloud and living smoke' — 'At a particular stage
of its flowering, a yew which bears male flowers, if struck, or
even if shaken strongly by the wind, will send up the pollen
(hence "fruitful", "living") in a "cloud" of yellow "smoke".'
And Bradley quotes a parallel passage from another poem by
Tennyson. The line 'And dippest toward the dreamless head'
shows, Bradley perspicaciously says, the change in feeling since
section II by its contrast with the line there 'Thy fibres net the
dreamless head.' For the gormless and perhaps the not so gormless,
he explains that the phrase 'the golden hour' means the Spring.
There are one or two other not superfluous notes, and they end
with a succinct discussion of the section's penultimate line: 'Thy
gloom is kindled at the tips.' The two views here are that the
phrase may refer either to the flowers or the shoots. Bradley

admits that the word 'tips' is 'by no means appropriate to the position of the flowers of the yew . . . But "kindled" is more appropriate to the flower than to the shoot, and the "point" that Sorrow has to meet concerns the flower.' He accordingly comes down on the side of flowers. Though he is almost certainly wrong here — having been seduced by the line 'When flower is feeling after flower' which I feel sure is merely intended to characterize the season and not to refer specifically to the yew tree — the lack of dogmatism and the presentation of the alternative enables him to perform a truly critical function. This is far from the setting-up of a row of Aunt Sallys, merely confusing to those after the coconuts.

Much of the foregoing may seem trivial in the extreme but my feeling is that the total meaning of the poem often resides in its details, the truth of which the poet is vitally concerned to preserve and to reconcile, an aim on which he is fixed throughout his successive drafts. Further work on a poem is, I think, often occasioned by the poet's sense that its internal logic still remains unsound, though the unsoundness could probably stay undiscovered after many readings from the outside. Indeed, it is this particular sense of unsatisfactoriness that prompts the poet to lavish work on the poem that brings rewards to it of quite different kinds.

In the Tennyson poem I don't feel any deficiency in its inner logic. The sexual characterization of Spring — 'When flower is feeling after flower' — is absolutely right realistically and for the sense of the poem, and the word 'flower' is not forced by either fact or the necessity of the rhyme. The fresh pale green growth at the tips of the branches certainly does take place during the Spring and, of course, eventually assumes the colour of the rest of the tree — and at this conclusion no extension of the flower metaphor is required by the concept of the poem nor do we feel it excluded by the exigency of the rhyme.

No doubt it may be said that it is easier to be a sensible critic faced by *In Memoriam* than by Dylan Thomas's 'Religious Sonnets'. But it is a reprehensible tendency of modern criticism,

confronted by the near baffling, to slip into the inclusively expository and to shirk its historical, biographical and evaluatory
functions. Needless to say the tendency is not confined to critics
of verse: examples may be culled almost weekly from writers on
art — 'Caro's sculpture turns the place into a steel-master's
elysium: although with no sense of either nature or engineering.
Neither *participation mystique* nor *technique* is invoked; nuts,
bolts, welding are simply part of a total effect. And these substantial metal objects are also events, iron idylls... Our first
responses are likely to be conceptual: general ideas — angularity,
poise, asymmetry — float into the mind. A few more inward,
more physical ones follow — pointing, leaning, impinging. The
beautiful piece from the Tate... works by offsetting the square
and heavy with the lyrical; the bending willowy tubes suggest
swaying or dancing... And yet for all their palpability and
weight these works do not invite physical responses. They often
point, spread, or even wander in various directions, so that it is
difficult to estimate how much space they are taking up... But
if they do little to create space, they occupy it in a disconcerting
way. Even walking round them is a problematic exercise. How
near should we go? Should we stop here? Is this the best place?
You don't want to get entangled with them — nor to bark your
shins. This "excluding" quality, keeping us at a distance, is
epitomised on the few occasions where a curved section is used.
It always seems placed in the interests of convexity rather than
concavity... What we notice most forcibly in all these works is
the business of joining. We follow their articulation, we record
their syntax. They offer the analytical pleasures of parsing them.
But more than that, they have an expressive "musical" quality;
we follow their development in time. We feel that they have
been made, not through adding one bit to another according to
a preconceived programme, but through a subjective involve-
ment, a process. In other words, they are the product of trial and
error. This perhaps accounts for a graceful, lively precariousness
in some of them. What leans plays an important role in Caro's
work.'

However, I must resist further quotation from this extraordinary but by no means untypical notice. Like Kleinman on the 'Religious Sonnets', its humourless exhaustiveness, its aim of saying all that can possibly be said about the art-object it confronts, pays scant regard, it seems to me, to either the artist's legitimacy of intention or the extent of his success. I know that the critic in the long run plays little or no part in the artist's organic development: all the same, much contemporary criticism would tend to fix an artist at any stage of inchoateness that caught the critic's fancy. I have heard a young poet say that the precise delineation of reality or emotion was superannuated, that the hint to the reader to work it out for himself was enough; and this view undoubtedly stems from the distrust of tropes, observation and description authorized by a certain critical school.

I have said or implied that a poem's legitimacy of reference or obscurity is directly related to its success. Of course, a poem's success may also turn on the legitimacy of its reference or obscurity, and I am necessarily ducking here the business of what makes a successful poem. But one believes, for example, without the researches and speculations of an Elder Olson or a Kleinman, that 'Gerontion' has earned its final puzzle:

> *What will the spider do,*
> *Suspend its operations, will the weevil*
> *Delay? De Bailhache, Fresca, Mrs Cammel, whirled*
> *Beyond the circuit of the shuddering Bear*
> *In fractured atoms.*

I don't say it wouldn't be interesting to know who De Bailhache, Fresca and Mrs Cammel were: it would merely be irrelevant.

I was brought up short in Oxford not long ago by a question at a meeting of a College literary society. Could I reasonably expect a reader to pick up the cultural references in my verse? The question has added point in these days when it is said that new readers may lack or renounce the culture which one imagined was part of the business of writing verse. Previously my poetic life has been spent in times when under Eliot's authority contemporary poetry was expected to be difficult, and under Auden's example was not likely to renounce the promptings of wide reading. And even before I'd ever heard of Auden the rediscovery of Donne and the other Metaphysicals had been made.

Betwixt mine eye and object, certain lines
Move in the figure of a pyramis,
Whose chapter in mine eye's gray apple shines,
The base within my sacred object is . . .

As for George Chapman and his successors, the terminology and discoveries of contemporary science have always seemed to me poetically usable and significant.

On the other hand, since the early 'thirties we have been more or less constantly aware of the contradiction between a poetry that claims a social function and an audience whose miniscule size is limited not only by its willingness to comprehend but also by its power. Even the few who discovered one's filthy aunts have seemed doomed to find them symbolic. The modes of poetry appear to an unusual degree baffling even to those who might be assumed to share the experience that goes to make it. Some critics, far from adding to modern poetry's esotericism, like Kleinman, have attempted to anatomize its difficulties, with a view to discarding the gratuitously opaque. The most able of them to my mind was the American, Yvor Winters. I think, for example, no poet who has read his *Primitivism and Decadence* can ever again embark light-heartedly on the category of pseudo-reference that Winters calls reference to a non-existent plot. The cast of De Bailhaches, Frescas and Mrs Cammels in contemporary verse was there pretty effectively limited.

Moreover, I think many poets, dreaming as poets do of a new start, a new period, a new style, covet greater simplicity either of language or theme or both. How, one enviously wonders, did they do it, those great simplifiers of the past — far from simple men creating with simple means verse of great resonance?

Three Virgins at the break of day:
"Whither, young Man, whither away?
"Alas for woe! alas for woe!"
They cry, & tears for ever flow.
The one was Cloth'd in flames of fire,
The other Cloth'd in iron wire,
The other Cloth'd in tears & sighs
Dazling bright before my Eyes.
They bore a Net of golden twine
To hang upon the Branches fine.
Pitying I wept to see the woe
That Love & Beauty undergo,
To be consum'd in burning Fires
And in ungratified desires,
And in tears cloth'd Night & day
Melted all my Soul away.
When they saw my Tears, a Smile
That did Heaven itself beguile,
Bore the Golden Net aloft
As on downy Pinions soft
Over the Morning of my day.
Underneath the Net I stray,
Now intreating Burning Fire,
Now intreating Iron Wire,
Now intreating Tears & Sighs.
O when will the morning rise?

One doesn't see, despite the fashionable highbrow taste for
pop lyrics, any resuscitation being valid of a simple and faintly
dotty symbolism. The Blakean method belongs firmly to a
happy epoch pre-psychoanalysis, pre-surrealism. And one must
add about Yvor Winters, however much sympathy one has for
his battle against the illegitimately obscure, that he was led
through his theories to champion a number of bloodless and
indubitably minor modern poets, and his own verse, though
technically fine, was colourless sometimes to the point of *ennui*.

One doesn't in fact, even under social systems where traditional culture is no longer a class prerogative, see any prospect of good poetry being in some way able to abandon the wealth of historical reference, the insights of science, the sophisticated vocabulary and syntax, that the centuries have accumulated. To take a relatively crude example: insofar as translations allow a judgment to be made, the methods of Voznesensky almost guarantee him to be a superior poet to Yevtushenko.

Besides, the oracular role of the poet — or, putting it less high-falutinly, poetry's puzzle element — is part of the game. The utterances of the Pythoness cannot be immediately intelligible: her warnings are always in advance of human conduct and understanding. Poets are not moralists or politicians — or entertainers.

But equally poets do not write for posterity. To come down to mundane cases, when I say 'The deep insensitive tissues of the heart' I want some readers to know that those tissues really are, literally are, insensitive, contrary to what sentiment would expect of the organ. It may be too much to hope yet that those trained in the Humanities will have dipped into a book on anatomy, but surely not that a few surgeons will be among one's readers. A literary critic complained recently that a phrase of mine — 'the purple colloids of the air' — was quite pleasant but imprecise. He had actually taken the trouble to look up the word 'colloid' and in fact quoted a meaning I intended: 'a non-crystalloid state of substance in suspension in water or alcohol which does not diffuse through parchment or a colloidal membrane.' He was merely unable to make the imaginative transference of colloids from a liquid to a gaseous medium, and had never had his eyes open in the quite common summer dusk the line was trying to pin down.

It was the same critic who quoted some lines of mine that I am prepared to defend as accurate if not as good poetry.

The image of a seabird
With scimitars of wings,

Pathetic feet tucked away,
A fine, ill-omened name,
Sweeping across the grey.

His comment was: 'Why are the feet "pathetic"? "Scimitars" may give the rough shape of the wings, and again it sounds good, but it gives too much else as well — what are the wings likely to cut? (surely not the air); are they really shiny and hard? If not, why are they made to seem so? And wouldn't it be better to know the bird's name, instead of being offered vague emotions about it?' I must say I would have thought the clue 'ill-omened bird with scimitar-like wings' a gift even for *The Times* crossword. Of course there one could have counted nine empty squares and that would also have been a help at arriving at the answer — surprise, surprise! — ALBATROSS. At the period the poem was written I had ample leisure to observe this creature while on watch in various troopships in the Southern Hemisphere, and I can assure those with less fortunate opportunities that its wings are so shaped. And though I don't press the point, which was not in mind, they do cut the air. In flight, the legs even of a sea-gull, which can be seen in this hemisphere, seem to me to be plausibly characterized as pathetic — through their size, position, function, and even colour.

All the same, one tips one's hat to, in the words of I. A. Richards, 'any expository work which comes sufficiently near its subject matter to run any risks'. Richards's remark comes from a piece of his originally published in the *Criterion*, a brilliant pendant to his *Practical Criticism*, which may now be conveniently read in his book *Speculative Instruments*. It is a piece about the diverse and often ludicrous results of asking his students to paraphrase fifteen lines from Landor's *Gebir*, and one of his conclusions is — obvious when made, but startling nonetheless — that 'any of these readers might discuss at length Landor's merits or defects as a poet, and even the qualities of this passage . . . without ever discovering the discrepancies of their reading.' And later he goes on to say: 'A judgment seemingly about a poem is primarily

4*

evidence about a reading of it . . . Every critical opinion is an ellipsis; a conditional assertion with the conditional part omitted. Fully expanded it would state that if a mind of a certain sort, under certain conditions (stage of its development, width of its recoverable experience, height of its temporary vigilence, direction of its temporary interest, etc), has, at scores, or hundreds, or thousands of points in the growth of its response to certain words, taken certain courses; then such and such. But, as a rule, it seems to be immediately about a certain fictional public object, a projected experience, the poem. It pretends to be, and is usually taken to be, a categoric assertion, discussable as though it were in simple logical relations, of agreement or contradiction and so on, with other assertions of the same type. But these also are collapsed conditional statements.'

Richards's essay makes two things plain: first, that wrong readings come not only from students but also, as I have been trying to demonstrate, from professional critics (he himself gives examples from Coleridge, H. W. Garrod and Rupert Brooke); and secondly, that in reading a poem, as he says, 'personal pre-occupations are strong enough to override everything and twist any pointers into directions governed by the reader's own volitional situation.' We can't wonder, with such evidence and such consideration in mind, at false poetic reputations, both of undervaluation and over-inflation, that so long and otherwise unaccountably persist.

Another question I've been asked in Oxford is whether I wouldn't like, whether it wouldn't be useful, to append notes to my verse. Again, the question, though simple, makes one ponder, especially being convinced that the questioner's tongue was a good way from his cheek. Certainly I have reason to dislike other people's notes, and I think my spot answer was to draw attention to the regrettable fate of the notes to *The Waste Land*, which have excited almost as much exegesis as the poem itself. It's true that those notes were not the most helpful, but in any case my sense is, as I hope I've implied this afternoon, that anything left over from the poem which really presses to be said is an indication of incomplete poetic success; and, on the other side of the medal, the work-task the poet legitimately imposes on the reader is all part of his effect, of the poem's effect.

I want to end with two critical remarks that have been favourites of mine for many years. The first is by Eliot: 'The possible interests of a poet are unlimited; the more intelligent he is the better; the more intelligent he is the more likely that he will have interests.' Poet-critics in their criticism are usually grinding the axe of their own poetry but here Eliot seems to me to be saying something that is universally true. It is also something that readers do not always see or admit, and it is a reason for poetry's native difficulty. And one might add that it is not contradicted by a saying of Dylan Thomas quoted by John Weightman in his inaugural lecture at Westfield College in the University of London in 1968 and which may gain currency: 'The bigger the fool, the better the poet.' Thomas, who whatever else may be said against him was certainly outstandingly intelligent in his sober years, I am sure was referring here to character not brain-power — the essential innocence in relation to experience and personal relations typical of many poets, a Parsifal-like chumpishness.

The other remark I want to quote is by Empson: 'The reasons that make a line of verse likely to give pleasure . . . are like the reasons for anything else.' I would want to substitute here some criterion other than the hedonistic one of 'pleasure' — as Yvor Winters has said, 'Milton did not write *Paradise Lost* to give pleasure to Professor so-and-so' — but again the basic thought seems to me unchallengeable and often forgotten. Even the great simple poets were formidably intelligent; and the reasons why their poetry — why all good poetry — rings the bell are not to be sought by crack-pot speculation or in magical mumbo-jumbo.

VI

How to Stuff Owls

In a lecture he gave in Paris in 1945, T. S. Eliot said that there were two kinds of bad poet — the 'faux mauvais', those who have a spurt of writing poetry in their youth, and the 'vrais mauvais', those who keep on writing it. In lecturer and audience this afternoon perhaps both kinds come together: at any rate I hope we shall find a common interest in bad poetry, to my mind a subject of importance.

The editors of the celebrated anthology of bad verse, *The Stuffed Owl*, also categorized the subject. They said in their preface that 'Bad Verse has its canons, like Good Verse. There is bad Bad Verse and good Bad Verse'; and they set out to include in their book chiefly good Bad Verse. The book was first published in 1930 and it is interesting to find how inadequate and outdated their definitions are, though their broad division is obviously useful. 'Good Bad Verse,' they said, 'is grammatical, it is constructed according to the Rubrics, its rhythms, rimes and metres are impeccable.' Neither editor, I think, had any sympathy with what was often still called in 1930 'modern' or 'modernist' poetry. 'A certain delicacy' they spoke of in their preface had excluded from the anthology 'many honoured names of the present moment', and, as they said, the enrichment of the book '(not to speak of its considerable enlargement) with extracts from eminent living English poets would not compensate the momentary hot embarrassment which would perhaps have followed' the request 'for permission to quote from their works'. One might guess that had the self-imposed ban been lifted and permission granted they would have included a good few verses now admired which in 1930 seemed decidedly rum to those whose taste had remained traditional; for example:

> Should I, after tea and cakes and ices,
> Have the strength to force the moment to its crisis.

Certainly were the anthology now brought up to date it would have to include bad verse that was ungrammatical, not constructed to any Rubrics capable of being systemized, with peccable rhymes, and quite *sui generis* as to rhythm and metre. The editors of *The Stuffed Owl* might have had difficulty in recognizing such bad verse as good Bad Verse: in any event it is plain they would have had to add to their recognition tests. The question of spotting good Bad Verse without the touchstone of skill in traditional forms is one that has grown more acute over the intervening years, and I shall be mentioning it again later.

As for bad Bad Verse, the discrimination of *The Stuffed Owl* editors must also strike the present reader as insufficiently refined. 'The field of bad Bad Verse,' they said in their facetious style, 'is vast, and confusing in its tropical luxuriance. The illiterate, the semi-literate, the Babu, the nature-loving contributor to the county newspaper, the retired station-master, the spinster lady coyly attuned to Life and Spring, the hearty but ill-equipped patriot, the pudibond yet urgent Sappho of endless *Keepsakes* and *Lady's Magazines* — nearly all those amateurs, inept for commerce with the Nine, who have ever attempted Parnassus (that is, about one-tenth of the average population of Empire) have been passed over, often with reluctance.' As a matter of fact, they don't — and it is reprehensible of them — adhere even to this rule. For instance, they actually print a couplet from a Babu poet on the death of Queen Victoria:

Dust to dust, and ashes to ashes,
Into the tomb the Great Queen dashes.

There the fault simply arises from the use of a thesaurus with an imperfect knowledge of the language, and not too much can be inferred of the poet's sensibility and intellect. The editors include, too, several poets who are really in the retired station-master or coy spinster lady class but who through unusual copiousness and persistence have achieved a wider fame. An example is Julia Moore, known as the Sweet Singer of Michigan, who died as recently as 1920. I quote the first stanza of her poem on Byron:

'Lord Byron' was an Englishman
  A poet I believe,
His first works in old England
  Was poorly received.
Perhaps it was 'Lord Byron's' fault
  And perhaps it was not.
His life was full of misfortunes,
  Ah, strange was his lot.

This is neither grammatically nor technically right. Julia Moore assorts no more than would William McGonagall with the principles enunciated by *The Stuffed Owl* editors. One may add also that it was quite unfair of them to include examples of un-conscious rudery — rudery resulting from the profane mind of the reader or an historical change in word usage — such as Henry Vaughan's line: 'How brave a prospect is a bright back-side!' And, of course, even less legitimate would have been examples of unconscious indelicacy which might have been incorporated had *The Stuffed Owl* appeared in a more permissive time; for example:

'The curse has come upon me,' cried
The Lady of Shalott.

However, today one would be troubled most with their notion that the productions of the illiterate or semi-illiterate must be automatically put in the class of bad Bad Verse. I'm not sure this was ever a well-enough defined proposition: there is a sense in which the dubieties in Keats, for example, seem to arise from semi-literacy:

> For, indeed, 'tis a sweet and peculiar pleasure
>   (And blissful is he who such happiness finds),
> To possess but a span of the hour of leisure,
>   In elegant, pure, and aerial minds.

This is from the rather obviously indifferent poem quoted in *The Stuffed Owl*: quite a few phrases could be detached from better works.

But now, of course, much admired verse is stuck in semi-literacy. For this, and for the reason of the decline in the use of traditional, skilled techniques, the categories of good Bad Verse and bad Bad Verse seem to me no longer to work. It might be preferable to use those of dangerous bad verse and harmless bad verse. In the latter category could be put all bad verse that is unlikely to be admired or imitated, from the work of the Sweet Singer of Michigan to the anonymous epitaphist in the local paper:

> Peacefully sleeping,
> No worry, no pain,
> God bless you dear
> Until we meet again.

In this category, too, I would feel bound to put certain poetic lapses like the notorious passage in Wordsworth's 'Vaudracour and Julia':

>   To a lodge that stood
> Deep in a forest, with leave given, at the age
> Of four-and-twenty summers he withdrew;
> And thither took with him his motherless Babe,

And one domestic for their common needs,
An aged woman. It consoled him here
To attend upon the orphan, and perform
Obsequious service to the precious child,
Which, after a short time, by some mistake
Or indiscretion of the Father, died.

The Stuffed Owl editors very rightly make much of this sort of obtuseness. It arises most often through too great a reliance by the poet on poetic theories. Wordsworth was convinced of the necessity for poetry to deal simply with domestic subjects (rather like the Movement poets of the 'fifties) and for this he is blameless, but he does not reckon on the ticklish effect of enclosing the subject in a framework of sub-Miltonic diction and inversions. One often sees the reverse kind of misjudgment in the simplicities of the *Lyrical Ballads*:

Full five-and-thirty years he lived
A running huntsman merry;
And though he has but one eye left,
His cheek is like a cherry.

But there is nothing evil in the conscious poetic effort here: on the contrary. And of course on a great many occasions Wordsworth balances admirably on the knife-edge.

It is with rather less confidence that we may categorize some Tennysonian lapses. The sentimentalities and ponderous thought movements were certainly widely imitated but they are rather features of the age than inheritable vices in the particular poet, and so much good work is there that we can indulgently leaf over such pages as:

O but she will love him truly!
  He shall have a cheerful home;
She will order all things duly,
  When beneath his roof they come.

Some of the early poems can only be excused if we think of

them as necessary exercises in the evolution of Tennyson's
marvellous metrical command:

> When my passion seeks
> Pleasance in love-sighs
> She, looking through and through me
> Thoroughly to undo me,
> Smiling, never speaks:
> So innocent-arch, so cunning-simple,
> From beneath her gathered wimple
> Glancing with black-beaded eyes,
> Till the lightning laughters dimple
> The baby-roses in her cheeks
> Then away she flies.

The ghastly progeny that such a style fathered inclines one to
put it in the more venal class.

Dangerous bad verse, then, is verse with a bad influence: it
would also be, in my definition, certain verse by over-valued
poets.

It is significant that no poem in *The Stuffed Owl* dates from earlier
than the second half of the seventeenth century. There are no
examples of bad verse from Surrey or Sackville, from Drayton
or Chapman, from Herbert of Cherbury or Drummond of
Hawthornden. In fact, even the seventeenth-century extracts
given won't, I think, seem to modern taste bad at all; rather the
reverse. Predictably, Cowley is the first poet in the book. One
of the two extracts by which he is represented is from his 'Ode
upon Dr Harvey' and the fact that this is also one of the two
poems of his in Auden and Pearson's four-volume anthology,
Poets of the English Language (published twenty-two years later
than *The Stuffed Owl*), is an amusing illustration of the re-
valuation of the metaphysical poets which was such an important
part of the revolution in poetry of this century, and which *The
Stuffed Owl* editors, with their 'traditional' views, were just
lagging behind. Cowley's celebration of the discoverer of the

circulation of the blood doesn't now, I think, appear in the least ludicrous; marvellous, rather:

> Before the Liver understood
> The noble Scarlet Dye of Blood,
> Before one drop was by it made,
> Or brought into it to set up the Trade;
> Before the untaught Heart began to beat
> The tuneful March to vital heat,
> From all the Souls that living Buildings rear,
> Whether imploy'd for Earth, or Sea, or Air,
> Whether it in the Womb or Egg be wrought,
> A strict account to him is hourly brought,
> How the great Fabrick does proceed,
> What Time, and what Materials it does need.
> He so exactly does the Work survey,
> As if he hir'd the Workers by the day.

And as for the extracts from the Duchess of Newcastle's poetry, for the ordinary reader these may be counted as a discovery comparable with the discovery of her contemporary, the American Edward Taylor, which also took place in the 'thirties, except that Taylor was uncovered by admirers. The talent has the inevitable tendency to excess and the domestic of most women poets, but the fancy is true and lively:

> Sweet marmalade of kisses newly gather'd,
> Preserved children, which were newly fathered,
> Sugar of beauty, which away melts soon,
> Marchpane of Youth, and childish macaroon:
> Sugar-plum words, which fall sweet from the lips,
> And water-promises mould'ring like chips;
> Biscuits of love which crumble all away,
> Jelly of Fear, which shak'd and quiv'ring lay:
> There was a fresh green-sickness cheese brought in,
> And tempting fruit, like that which Eve made sin.

Certainly the hyperbole of the later Metaphysicals becomes increasingly outrageous and less and less felt, the danger of sinking being therefore always present. Our anthologists were quite right, for example, to include such things as this from Richard Blackmore:

With teats distended with their milky store,
Such num'rous lowing herds, before my door,
Their painful burden to unload did meet,
That we with butter might have wash'd our feet.

But Blackmore died as late as 1729 and is duly enshrined in *The Dunciad*. The eighteenth century is, of course, a rich source of legitimate material for *The Stuffed Owl*. This rather sudden availability of English poetry for the purposes of mockery irresistibly calls to mind the famous passage in T. S. Eliot's essay, 'The Metaphysical Poets'. That essay, written in 1921, took the form of a review of Grierson's *Metaphysical Lyrics and Poems of the Seventeenth Century*, itself a landmark in the formation of our present opinion of the poetry of that period. It will be remembered that in the essay Eliot is comparing Chapman with Browning, Herbert of Cherbury with Tennyson, to the disadvantage of the later poets so far as concerns 'a direct sensuous apprehension of thought, or a recreation of thought into feeling'. Then Eliot goes on:

The difference is not a simple difference of degree between poets. It is something which had happened to the mind of England between the time of Donne or Lord Herbert of Cherbury and the time of Tennyson and Browning; it is the difference between the intellectual poet and the reflective poet. Tennyson and Browning are poets, and they think; but they do not feel their thought as immediately as the odour of a rose. A thought to Donne was an experience; it modified his sensibility. When a poet's mind is perfectly equipped for its work, it is constantly amalgamating disparate experience; the ordinary man's experience is chaotic, irregular, fragmentary. The latter falls in love, or reads Spinoza, and these two experiences have nothing to do with each other, or with the noise of the typewriter or the smell of cooking; in the mind of the poet these experiences are always forming new wholes.

We may express the difference by the following theory: The poets of the seventeenth century, the successors of the dramatists of the sixteenth, possessed a mechanism of sensibility which could devour any kind of experience. They are simple, artificial, difficult, or fantastic, as their predecessors were . . . In the seventeenth century a dissociation of sensibility sets in, from which we have never recovered; and this dissociation, as is natural, was aggravated by the influence of the two most powerful poets of the century, Milton and Dryden. Each of these men performed certain poetic functions so magnificently well that the magnitude of the effect concealed the absence of others. The language went on and in some respects improved; the best verse of Collins, Gray, Johnson, and even Goldsmith satisfies some of our fastidious demands better than that of Donne or Marvell or King. But while the language became more refined, the feeling became more crude. The feeling, the sensibility, expressed in the Country Churchyard *(to say nothing of Tennyson and Browning) is cruder than that in the* Coy Mistress.

The second effect of the influence of Milton and Dryden followed from the first, and was therefore slow in manifestation. The sentimental age began early in the eighteenth century, and continued. The poets revolted against the ratiocinative, the descriptive; they thought and felt by fits, unbalanced; they reflected. In one or two passages of Shelley's Triumph of Life, *and in the second* Hyperion, *there are traces of a struggle toward unification of sensibility. But Keats and Shelley died, and Tennyson and Browning ruminated.*

Whatever damage may have been done to this theory by later critics (including Eliot himself) it holds up remarkably well in the field of bad verse. Reading *The Stuffed Owl* on the eighteenth and nineteenth centuries, we must sense the tendency of poets to brainlessness in their art. At random one lights, for instance, on these lines on climbing the Malvern Hills by Joseph Cottle, the bookseller friend of Coleridge and Wordsworth:

Still I toil.
How long and steep and cheerless the ascent!
It needs the evidence of close deduction
To know that I shall ever reach the height!

One sees clearly, too, the extreme difficulty those poets had of sensibly combining low things and high things, love and the smell of cooking. Here is Leigh Hunt on the first meeting alone of Paolo and Francesca:

'*May I come in?' said he: — it made her start, —*
That smiling voice; — she colour'd, pressed her heart
A moment, as for breath, and then with free
And usual tone said, — 'O yes, certainly.'

This difficulty persisted until our own century: in a letter of 1905 W. B. Yeats wrote that he was 'now correcting the last few lines [of *The Shadowy Waters*], and have joyfully got "creaking shoes" and "liquorice-root" into what has been a very abstract passage.'

And, as T. S. Eliot said, sentimentality set in very early, and one may think that *The Stuffed Owl* editors don't make quite enough of this prime source of badness in verse, though it does, of course, take space to illustrate.

After the seventeenth-century examples there are only two poets in *The Stuffed Owl* who seem to us now unfairly pilloried. They are both of the eighteenth century and it is not entirely an accident that they were both physicians. John Armstrong is undoubtedly the lesser of the two, and possibly I'm inclined to overvalue his long poem, the *Art of Preserving Health*, because I've not always found my own easy to preserve. One of *The Stuffed Owl* extracts remarkably anticipates a modern theory (the correctness of which I firmly believe) about the formation of peptic ulcers — the chemical effect on the stomach lining when the stomach acid encounters the bile, hence the value of a low-fat diet for sufferers — but quite apart from this extrinsic interest the passage is far from badness:

The languid stomach curses even the pure
Delicious fat, and all the race of oil:
For more the oily aliments relax
Its feeble tone; and with the eager lymph
(Fond to incorporate with all it meets)
Coyly they mix, and shun with slippery wiles
The woo'd embrace. The irresoluble oil,
So gentle late and blandishing, in floods
Of rancid bile o'erflows: what tumults hence,
What horrors rise, were nauseous to relate.
Choose leaner viands, ye whose jovial make
Too fast the gummy nutriment imbibes.

Critics have often noted the power of Erasmus Darwin — he is in Geoffrey Grigson's fine anthology, *The Romantics*, for instance — and several of the extracts by which he is represented in *The Stuffed Owl* are quite remarkable in the best sense:

Allied to fish, the Lizard cleaves the flood,
With one-cell'd heart, and dark frigescent blood;
Half-reasoning Beavers long-unbreathing dart
Through Eirie's waves with perforated heart;
With gills and lungs respiring Lampreys steer,
Kiss the rude rocks, and suck till they adhere;
With gills pulmonic breathes th'enormous Whale,
And spouts aquatic columns to the gale.

With Eliot's dissociation of sensibility there also set in what may be called a dissociation of labour: poets became men of letters. The two processes are not disconnected and their underlying causations are similar. The work of John Armstrong and Erasmus Darwin shows the great advantage to poetry, when it ventures into realms beyond the poet's immediate observation and feelings, of a body of practical learning. Poets also became women — and women also without other than domestic occupations. There is no discrimination against women in *The Stuffed Owl*.

In their preface, *The Stuffed Owl* editors educe bathos as the predominating quality that makes bad verse bad but of course their notion of what is bathetic is governed by their notion of what is poetic. Eliot long ago accustomed us to corsets and the yellow soles of feet as proper poetic properties; and subsequent critics such as Geoffrey Grigson have made us value accuracy to nature so highly that some of us find almost intrinsically poetic any scientific observation, even of bile or beavers. The compiler of a collection of bad verse today would find the bathetic a much more limited source of material.

The other broad category of bad verse in *The Stuffed Owl* is what the editors call 'windy splurging and bombinating', often, they point out, allied to false patriotism. Our new anthologist would certainly find it easy to include examples of windy splurging and bombinating but the greater cunning and sophistication of poets have for a long time avoided false patriotism. Inflated and noisy verse on public themes could still be discovered but it would have to be drawn from such work as Viet Nam protest poetry.

One thing a new anthologist would want to make clear — *The Stuffed Owl* demonstrates it unconsciously — is how from time to time in English poetry a school of poets arises which despises the intellect and elevates the feelings. The Della Cruscans at the end of the eighteenth century, the Spasmodics in the middle of the nineteenth — and in our own day the New Apocalyptics of the 'forties and that beat or underground movement unfortunately still with us: all these produced an amount of dangerous bad verse. It would be tedious and probably superfluous to document it: besides, I want to try if I can to emulate *The Stuffed Owl* editors' delicacy in refraining from quoting living poets. The attitude behind it at every period seems to be the strange notion that intellectual power inhibits valuable feeling, though that the precise contrary is true must be evident, at least to those with intellects. The expression of the notion in our time was pithily, if illiterately, put by a student at the Hornsey College of Art, an anonymous contributor to the Penguin Educational Special,

The Hornsey Affair, an account of the revolt in the College in 1968: 'Our anti- or a-intellectualism was compensated by more intact senses.'

Of course, it hardly needs to be said that the intellect cannot be abolished, even in Hornsey. Homo sapiens must to some degree be sapiens. The artistic products of the anti-intellectuals are appreciated through the intellect. So, the great reputations and often long-enduring work of bad poets parody the reputations and work of good poets. The eminence of the bad is by no means merely the result of popular applause. The dangerously bad poet at the vital stage of his career is usually taken up by respectable critical opinion. We sometimes forget how high and seemingly unassailable certain poetic reputations have been. The author of *Festus* comes to mind, and the Edwardian poet Stephen Phillips. Of Philip James Bailey a writer as eminent as Harrison Ainsworth said: 'His place will be among the first, if not the first, of our native poets.' And at the back of the fourteenth edition of Phillips's *Poems* there is a quotation from a review in *The Times* which assigned to that now completely unread book 'the indefinable quality which makes for permanence'.

When Macaulay mounted his celebrated attack on Robert Montgomery in 1830, Montgomery's poem *The Omnipresence of the Deity* was in its eleventh edition. Macaulay's essay had little immediate effect: twenty-eight years later there had been twenty-eight editions. The Oxford academic who edited Macaulay in the early days of this century deplored the essay and wished that it might have been allowed to drop out of the collected works: 'Serenely to ignore what is worthless and to fix his own attention and the attention of others upon what is precious — this is the wisdom of a critic as well as the instinct of a humane nature.' But this was said when Montgomery's fame had been safely extinguished. I hold strongly myself that Macaulay's destructive piece was not only timely but is also still of value. For one thing, the technical basis of the attack, though elementary, is too little applied: Macaulay demolishes Montgomery simply by demonstrating the often absurd ambiguity of his syntax and the imprecision of his imagery. For another, what Macaulay says about fashionable puffing and the operation of unargued critical opinion is still germane to the literary situation. And he himself adequately answered in the essay itself his later editor (it was F. C. Montague): 'Those who are best fitted to guide public opinion think it beneath them to expose mere nonsense, and comfort themselves by reflecting that such popularity cannot last. This contemptuous lenity has been carried too far. It is perfectly true that reputations which have been forced into an unnatural bloom fade almost as soon as they have been expanded; nor have we any apprehensions that puffing will ever raise any scribbler to the rank of a classic ... But ... we still think its influence most pernicious. Men of real merit will, if they persevere, at last reach the station to which they are entitled, and intruders will be ejected with contempt and derision. But it is no small evil that the avenues to fame should be blocked up by a swarm of noisy, pushing, elbowing pretenders, who, though they will not ultimately be able to make good their own entrance, hinder, in the mean time, those who have a right to enter. All who will not disgrace themselves by joining in the unseemly scuffle must expect to be at first hustled and shouldered back. Some men of talents, accordingly, turn away in dejection from pursuits in which success appears to bear no proportion to desert. Others employ in self-defence the means by which competitors, far inferior to themselves, appear for a time to obtain a decided advantage. There are few who have sufficient confidence in their own powers and sufficient elevation of mind to wait with secure and contemptuous patience, while dunce after dunce presses before them. Those who will not stoop to the baseness of the modern fashion are too often discouraged. Those who do stoop to it are always degraded.'

I was surprised not long ago to be chided by a writer in *Isis* (11 October, 1969) for saying that a critic's job was (as he put it) 'to tell us what's good and what's bad'. This seems to me a vestigial attitude: it reminded me of the remark made to a previous occupant of this Chair when he appeared before his

College board at the end of his first term as an Oxford undergraduate in 1919: 'I understand, Mr Graves, that the essays which you write for your English tutor are, shall I say, a trifle temperamental. It appears, indeed, that you prefer some authors to others.'

It is not unexpected that the poetry of feeling today, looking for ancestors, should light on William Blake. But what is curious is that Blake's work should have been accepted *in toto*. He is very obviously two poets: there is the pretty consistently high-class poet of strict forms, in the early work, even, inheriting the pedestrianism of the previous period; and there is the poet of the Prophetic Books. The latter poet is a very variable writer, but even those who, like me, do not relish his matter and manner are forced to recognize their marvellous parts. It is significant that those parts come largely when the metrics of the Prophetic Books were still more or less regular. Curious that Blake should have initially chosen the fourteener for these works, a stubbornly difficult line to handle; even more curious that his fourteeners should have been unrhymed, thus increasing the task of making the metre sound sensible, though of course making it technically easier to turn out. But the discipline certainly keeps the rhetoric within decent bounds; I quote from *The Book of Thel*:

> "*Then if thou art the food of worms, O virgin of the skies,*
> "*How great thy use, how great thy blessing! Every thing that lives*
> "*Lives not alone nor for itself. Fear not, and I will call*
> "*The weak worm from its lowly bed, and thou shalt hear its voice.*
> "*Come forth, worm of the silent valley, to thy pensive queen*"

The loosening of the fourteener and the introduction of other irregularities roughly corresponds with the increasing windy splurging and bombinating of the Prophetic Books. This intimate connection between form and content seems lost on many present-day Blake idolators. The editor of the Penguin anthology of the 'Poetry of the "Underground" in Britain' — a collection actually called, after Blake, *Children of Albion* — claims 'through Ginsberg . . . the heritage of Blake', but the heritage is without real technical control; only the indulgent rhetoric remains.

I connect — possibly without real justification — the bad side of Blake's verse with the anti-rationalist side of his thought. I've always felt uneasy about his animadversions on Newton and Joshua Reynolds, even when I was young enough not to feel the need of braces, and uneasier still when similar sentiments have been taken up by later poets. A thesis could very reasonably be propounded of bad literary art stemming from the aspect of Romanticism that despised science, a thesis that would take in the streak in Keats that soppily objected to the prismatic analysis of the rainbow and wind up with D. H. Lawrence and a number of American poets, a nation particularly prone to the disease. Lawrence, indeed, is almost as distinct a double-poet as Blake. Coming back to his verse, as I did recently after an interval of nearly forty years, an interval resulting from a shattered love affair with his work, I must say I was astonished at the effort and skill behind the earlier rhymed poems — a sustained labour which in my opinion raises them to a high place in the century's poetry. When his free verse style sets in — and it is connected with both a personal and philosophical indulgence — there is a marked lowering of achievement, despite the many marvels in such things as the *Birds, Beasts and Flowers* series. Here, almost at random, is the start of a rhymed poem, from Lawrence's days as a schoolmaster:

A faint, sickening scent of irises
Persists all morning. Here in a jar on the table
A fine proud spike of purple irises
Rising up in the class-room litter, makes me unable
To see the class's lifted and bended faces
Save in a broken pattern, amid purple and gold and sable.

And here from a far more celebrated poem is what seems to me a tedious repetitiveness and imprecision permitted by his very free free verse:

A fine wind is blowing the new direction of Time.
If only I let it bear me, carry me, if only it carry me!

If only I am sensitive, subtle, oh, delicate, a winged gift!
If only, most lovely of all, I yield myself and am borrowed
By the fine, fine wind that takes its course through the chaos
                                        of the world
Like a fine, an exquisite chisel, a wedge–blade inserted;
If only I am keen and hard like the sheer tip of a wedge
Driven by invisible blows,
The rock will split, we shall come at the wonder, we shall find
                                        the Hesperides.

Obviously I'm not insisting on rhyme as an essential stiffener
for a tendency to flabby romanticism. Indeed, in the case of E. E.
Cummings the romanticism that was kept fairly reasonably within
bounds by the arduous typographical preoccupations of his *vers libre*
runs quite wild when he comes to write his later rollicking stanzas:

so world is a leaf so tree is a bough
(and birds sing sweeter
than books
tell how)
so here is away and so your is a my
(with a down
up
around again fly)
forever was never till now . . .

we're anything brighter than even the sun
(we're everything greater
than books
might mean)
we're everyanything more than believe
(with a spin
leap
alive we're alive)
we're wonderful one times one.

Note in this *Stuffed Owl* stuff the sinister relegation of books:
'birds sing sweeter than books tell how'. It is simply not true: our

intenser appreciation of bird-song comes from the spade-work of field-workers who have identified it and categorized its various uses and occasions. And the proposition that the lovers are 'everything greater than books might mean', I'd like to return to later in a different context.

Technical deficiencies put us on warning of possible badness: so, too, must the absence of realistic connotations. The sentence with which Geoffrey Grigson ended his introduction to the anthology he made in 1939 of poems from his magazine *New Verse* put the latter point in a way which is perhaps over-rigorous but still useful: 'I judge every poem written now, by poets under forty, by the degree to which it takes notice, for ends not purely individual, of the universe of objects and events.'

Looking at my own bad poems — if I may immodestly assume that some are worse than others — I've often wondered what precisely made them bad. The bad ones (unless they are particularly inept) are not always easy to recognize at first, perhaps because they may start off with a donnée not in itself unpromising. Not long ago I came across such a poem in a file of old typescripts and recalled its immediate inspiration, which was the reading somewhere of the mediaeval belief that human character could be divided into four 'humours' — the sanguine, the phlegmatic, the choleric and the melancholy — and that the humour was determined by the preponderance of the particular secretion that governed it, blood determining the sanguine, phlegm the phlegmatic, yellow bile the choleric, black bile the melancholy. I wrote the poem in three ten-line stanzas of heroic couplets, and it begins reasonably enough:

Blood, phlegm, or yellow or black bile
Determines the human creature and his style.

I couldn't understand why it came back from the, perhaps, two or three editors I sent it to. Of course, now, some twenty years after, I see crudities of expression that could fairly easily be rectified. But even so the diction would still remain too clotted and, worse, its rhetoric is unrescuably unanchored to concrete experience, and its imagery is too much that of metaphor, too little that of simile. I'll bring myself to quote a few lines from the middle of the poem as a warning:

> The sinister shades of jealousy or Nurse
> Fall on three decades of unhappy verse.
> The wind turns over one more fatal page
> And passion beats the padded flesh of age.
> The cruelty of men the virtuous man
> Conceals in his indifferent mask. The plan
> Of perfect physical or urban cells
> Collapses in a sport of rubble, smells.

One can also detect here those other characteristics of bad verse, over-plus feelings and the poem imagining itself to be smarter than it really is.

It must be admitted that some bad verse — to an extent the very kind of my last few examples — has behind it the right poetic instinct. Plainly the intellectual element, even the technical element, on both of which I've been insisting, is in the final analysis subservient to the verbal element. A fine and sober critic, the late George Rostrevor Hamilton, who certainly could not be accused ever of neglecting intellect and technique, put the matter excellently in his book *Guides and Marshals*. He begins, in this passage, by quoting a line and a half from *Macbeth*:

> Duncan is in his grave;
> After life's fitful fever he sleeps well.

'Here,' he says, 'the idea contained — the parallel between natural sleep that comes to the solace of fever and natural death that brings relief from all the ills by which life can be harassed — is doubtless a true idea. But its value, however vividly realized, is very slight compared with the whole experience which the words in their context give. For words at the service of poetic genius transcend any idea which they contain: here they give us an exaltation for which life without those words holds no equivalent.'

Then he goes on to say this: 'I do not wish to undervalue the true ideas which may be won from poetry, ideas now lying near the surface and now only to be extracted by deep mining. In particular, I would not deny that they help in a measure to induce order in our minds. Yet, even in a poem like *The Pulley*' — he is referring to George Herbert's poem — 'the ideas which it *contains* . . . are a very secondary matter compared with the *whole* experience which we receive from it. I suggest, in short, that *the essential aim and achievement of poetry are not to discover existing truth, but to create new experience: experience, the elements of which are knit together through the medium of words in a much closer union than the patterns of ordinary life can show: experience, therefore, forming centres of more than usual order, the influence of which may spread through the whole mind or spirit.*'

And later, anticipating the criticism that he might be over-stressing the art of words, he says that 'a poet is set apart from other men, and other artists, precisely by his passion for words'.

It seems to me that part of the popularity of a bad poet like Robert Montgomery was a consequence of the general recognition that he had, after all, a passion for words. I take a couplet quoted in the Macaulay essay:

And thou, vast Ocean, on whose awful face
    Time's iron feet can print no ruin-trace.

I think one can see very well the superficial attraction of a line like 'Time's iron feet can print no ruin-trace.' All those editions were required before it sunk in that however reverberant or unusual the words were in the line, it was utterly arbitrary to ascribe iron feet to Time, and that the 'ruin-trace' of those feet — presumably Montgomery had some oxidization metaphor in mind — quite obviously couldn't in any event be printed on the ocean, though the plausibleness is vaguely sustained by the knowledge that sea-water does rust iron. The same sort of process may be seen in the work of the Apocalyptic poets of the 'forties

and in those poems of Dylan Thomas which were so largely the
source of their inspiration:

> *The mouth of time sucked, like a sponge,*
> *The milky acid on each hinge,*
> *And swallowed dry the waters of the breast.*

In Thomas the delusive process was assisted by his own
reading aloud, which emphasized the verbal element. Hence,
in a period such as ours of the poetry-recital and the long-playing
gramophone record, the increasing dangers of being dazzled by
mere words. The value of poetry should always be checked, away
from its noise, by a consideration of its logic and technique.

Another point that needs to be made if one isn't to condemn
oneself as wholly heartless, is that though bad verse results, the
impulse behind it may be humanly generous, historically forward-
looking. I was very struck recently by a casual remark made to
me in conversation by Jack Lindsay to the effect that the Spasmodics were the less-successful English equivalent of Baudelaire —
their work an attempt to bring the terrors and pities of the
modern '*fourmillante cité*' into poetry. I wish he would work out
this interesting notion, which my memory has necessarily
garbled. His words certainly reminded me that there is perhaps
no more dangerous badness than the badness of an outworn
poetic establishment. For instance, as T. S. Eliot said in 1954,
'The situation of poetry in 1909 or 1910 was stagnant to a degree
difficult for any young poet of today to imagine.' The chapter
in C. K. Stead's excellent book, *The New Poetic*, where these
words are used as an epigraph, clearly shows that the bad verse
of the earlier part of this century arose as much from its acceptance of bourgeois values as from its tame following of Victorian
diction. Had there been, in 1909 or 1910, a merely ideological
revolution in poetry rather than the largely technical one of
Eliot and Pound, who can doubt that great good would have
been done, even though the result, in poetic terms, had been little
more successful than the work of the Spasmodics.

Poets other than Blake and Lawrence are two poets: one thinks
of Keats and Shelley, Wordsworth and Tennyson. Perhaps this
too is a consequence of the dissociation of sensibility, for one
doesn't find the same Jekyll and Hyde character in earlier poets.
Other factors enter into the question, like the increasing expectation of life, a peril that modern poets are particularly susceptible
to, though war has redressed the situation somewhat. Like a few
other things, poetry is not necessarily an activity one gets better
at as one gets older. I may quote here a poem of my own actually
called 'The Two Poets':

The one was witty and observant,
Words and translucent form his servant.
The other counted beats, weighed vowels,
His verse as thick and coiled as bowels.

The first died young. The second aged,
And, though officially he raged
Against the former, privately
Envied the light lost poetry.

Envied but never ceased to hope,
Thinking it still within his scope,
That unsought carelessness and truth
— The lucky manner of his youth.

Lightness: there is no doubt that much of the badness in *The
Stuffed Owl* — and bad verse generally — arises from too solemn
a notion of poetry's function by those unable to sustain the notion.
What a relief it was and what a blessing — however often one's
forgotten the message in the interim — to come across in one's
early days as a poet the famous words in the introduction to
Auden and Garrett's anthology *The Poet's Tongue*: 'Everything
that we remember no matter how trivial: the mark on the wall,
the joke at luncheon, word games, these, like the dance of a
stoat or the raven's gamble, are equally the subject of poetry.

'We shall do poetry a great disservice if we confine it only to
the major experiences of life:

5

The soldier's pole is fallen,
Boys and girls are level now with men,
And there is nothing left remarkable
Beneath the visiting moon.

They had a royal wedding.
All his courtiers wished him well.
The horses pranced and the dancers danced.
O Mister it was swell.

And masculine is found to be
Hadria the Adriatic Sea,

have all their rightful place, and full appreciation of one depends on full appreciation of the others.'

I'd like to perorate by reading a fuller passage from *The Hornsey Affair*, the passage from which I drew my original quotation:

> *In western countries over the last few years, there has been a changing climate of sensibility, a large-scale cultural change, of which we were the inheritors and would eventually be the producers. This cultural change has far-reaching social and psychological consequences for art students and is one principal factor in explaining our unique position among students both before and after 28 May, which made that day possible. We suffered less from the castration of our sensibilities than many university students and other political groups. Our anti- or a-intellectualism was compensated by more intact senses. Our boldness was founded on our lack of "knowledge". We had not learned to live the present through books.*

As E. E. Cummings's poem said: 'We're everything greater than books might mean.'

The misconceptions here would be comic were they not pathetic. For isn't it precisely from our inheritance of the stock of good art — from 'the tradition' — that our sensibilities are able to operate in any refined or penetrating way? And not merely that: surely it is only by entering into the tradition, amplifying and (if we are unusually talented) extending it, that our own sensibilities can be properly expressed. The hall-marks of crude sensibility, of bad art, are — as I hope I've shown in the field of poetry — technical misconceptions, inaccurate expression and unobservant feeling. If there is one thing *The Stuffed Owl* shows and our own experience confirms above all else it is that mere feeling is too easy.

It would be superfluous to dilate on present-day art's decline in skill and subtlety. One wonders if the so-called 'cultural change' referred to by the Hornsey student and other recent writers isn't just a surrender to the infantile, the bathetic, the first thought, the popular inanities, which the best critics have always devoted much energy towards extirpating. If Hornsey had its way the prospect would open up of a culture in which not only the productions of the present were valued for the wrong reasons — as often in China or the Soviet Union — but also the art of the past totally misjudged; in which the skilled stanzas and couplets of Blake were forgotten and the incoherence of the later Prophetic Books imitated; the practice of the author of the *Cantos* unquestioningly accepted, his rigorous precepts rejected; the discipline of *Portrait of the Artist as a Young Man* neglected, the linguistic indulgences of *Finnegan's Wake* feebly employed. The perspective would narrow to a time when all anthologies would unwittingly be *Stuffed Owls*.

Index

Alvarez, A, 94–95
Apocalyptic Poets, 37, 119, 127
Armstrong, John, 117–18
Arnold, Matthew, 9, 10, 11, 15, 16, 17, 18, 21, 22, 23, 24, 25, 71
    Culture and Anarchy, 9, 10, 18
Arnold, Thomas, 18
Auden, W. H., 30, 53, 54, 58, 59, 60, 64, 102, 113, 129
    Another Time, 52
    'Consider', 94–95, 97
    Dyer's Hand, The, 52
    'Epilogue', 52
    'Heavy Date', 52
    'In Memory of Sigmund Freud', 51
    'Spain', 52

Bailey, Philip James, 120
Beatles, The, 15
Blackmore, Richard, 115
Blake, William, 96, 122, 123, 129, 131

Book of Thel, The, 122
    'Golden Net, The', 103
Blank verse, 46, 53, 57–61, 65
Bond, James, 14
Bradley, A. C., 95–96
    Commentary on Tennyson's In Memoriam, 97–99
Bradley, Henry (F. H.), 81
Bridges, Robert, 44, 45, 46, 59, 61, 65, 81

Cambridge, 27, 30, 60
Caro, Anthony, 100
Caudwell, Christopher, 33
Chapman, George, 102
Children of Albion, 122
Church, Henry, 70, 71
Cooke, Catherine, 96
Cottle, Joseph, 116–17
Cowley, Abraham, 113–14
Creeley, Robert, 39

Criterion, The, 61
Cummings, E. E., 124, 130

Daryush, Elizabeth, 44, 45, 53, 57, 58, 59, 64, 65–68
Last Man and Other Verses, The, 47
Verses, Fourth Book, 44, 48
Della Cruscans, 119
Donne, John, 102, 115

Eliot, T. S., 22, 46, 50, 58, 63, 72, 76, 102, 107, 108, 115–16, 117, 118, 128
'Gerontion', 101, 102
'Love Song of J. Alfred Prufrock, The', 109
Waste Land, The, 106
Empson, William, 91, 107
End-stopping, 57, 67

Faber Book of Modern Verse, The, 36
Free verse, 46, 53, 63–64, 123, 124
Freud, Sigmund, 51, 52, 73
Fyvel, T. R., 12

Galsworthy, John, 12
Germany, 20, 21, 24
Gide, André, 73
Ginsberg, Allen, 122
Gombrich, E. H., 16
Graves, Robert, 122
Grigson, Geoffrey, 30, 33, 85, 86–88, 119
New Verse, 30, 85, 125
Romantics, The, 118

Hamilton, George Rostrevor, 126–127
H.D. (Hilda Doolittle), 44, 46

Herbert, George, 127
Hitler, Adolf, 20
Hopkins, G. M., 61, 66
Hornsey College of Art, 119–20, 130, 131
Hough, Graham, 63–64
Housman, A. E.,
Name of Nature of Poetry, The, 60, 61, 62
Hunt, Leigh, 117

Isis, 121

James, Henry, 53, 59
Johnson, Samuel, 58, 60

Keats, John, 111, 116, 123, 129
Kermode, Frank, 81, 82, 84
Kleinman, H. H.,
Religious Sonnets of Dylan Thomas, The, 92–93, 96, 101, 102

Landor, W. S., 105
Lang, Andrew, 75
Latin, 23, 63, 66–67
Lawrence, D. H., 21, 29, 72, 123, 129
Lenin, V. I.,
'*Left Wing Communism': an Infantile Disorder,* 20
Levi, Peter, 66
Lindsay, Jack, 128
Liverpool Poets, The, 14, 41, 42
London Magazine, The, 53, 95
Love, Love, Love, 35
Lucie-Smith, Edward, 41

Macaulay, Thomas Babington, 120–21, 127
Macbeth, 55, 126

McGonagall, William, 110
Maoism, 18
Marxism, 30, 33, 49, 97
Metaphysicals, The, 102, 113, 115
Milton, John, 45, 46, 61, 65, 66, 116
  Paradise Lost, 59, 60, 95, 107
Montgomery, Robert, 120–21, 127
Moore, Julia, 110, 111
Moore, Marianne, 44–46 pass.
  'Buffalo, The', 48
  'Carriage from Sweden, A', 55
  Collected Poems, 1951, 48
  Complete Poems, 65
  'In Distrust of Merits', 56
  'Jerboa, The', 56
  'My Crow Pluto', 49
  Selected Poems, 1935, 48
  'Snakes, Mongooses, Snake
  Charmers and the Like', 50
  'Steeple-Jack, The', 47
  'To a Prize Bird', 56–57
Movement, The, 34, 112
Murray, The, 34, 112
Murray, Gilbert, 96

Newcastle, Duchess of, 114

Olson, Charles, 38, 39, 58, 64
Olson, Elder,
  Poetry of Dylan Thomas, The, 91–92,
  101
Oxford, 9, 16, 17, 21, 23, 101, 106,
  120

Paris Review, 45
Patten, Brian, 34, 35
Penguin Modern Poets, 40
Phillips, Stephen, 120
Pound, Ezra, 45, 46, 61–62, 128

Cantos, 22, 26, 131
Pavannes and Divisions, 46
Projective Verse, 38, 39, 41, 58, 62

Quarterly Review of Literature, 48

Reader's Guide to W. H. Auden, A, 95
Realism, 32, 33, 42, 82–84
Richards, I. A., 28, 29, 30, 31, 32, 33
  Practical Criticism, 27, 28, 29, 30, 42,
  43, 90, 105
  Speculative Instruments, 105–106
Rilke, R. M., 82, 83, 84

Schulman, Grace, 48, 50, 51
Science, 32, 33, 102, 104
Sentimentality, 28–43 pass., 117
Shelley, P. B., 129
Sitwell, Edith, 93
Socialism, 18, 25, 31, 32
Soviet Union, 23, 131
Spasmodics, 119, 128
Stead, C. K., 128
Stevens, Wallace, 69–88 pass.,
  Adagia, 86
  Auroras of Autumn, 79
  Collected Poems, 80, 85
  'Comedian as the Letter C, The', 76
  'Green Plant, The', 84–85
  Harmonium, 75, 77, 88
  Ideas of Order, 85, 86, 88
  Letters, 69–88 pass.
  Necessary Angel, The, 81
  'Notes Toward a Supreme Fiction',
  82
  'Of Hartford in a Purple Light',
  78–79
  Selected Poems, 83
  'Sunday Morning', 75

Stockhausen, Karlheinz, 15
Stuffed Owl, The, 108–31 *pass.*
Swift, Jonathan, 22
 Battle of the Books, The, 10
Syllabic verse, 44–68 *pass.*
Symons, Julian,
 Twentieth Century Verse, 37, 85

Tate, Allen, 64
Television, 12, 18
Tennyson, Alfred Lord, 112–13, 115,
 129
 In Memoriam, 97–99
 'Lady of Shalott, The', 110
Thomas, Dylan, 34, 37, 76, 107, 128
 'Altarwise by owl-light', 91–95, 96,
 99
 'Fern Hill', 34
 'Poem in October', 34, 41
 Deaths and Entrances, 33
Times, The, 14, 16, 105
Times Literary Supplement, The, 26, 86
Trilling, Lionel, 10

Vaughan, Henry, 110
Verse, technicalities of, *see* Blank verse
 End-stopping, Free verse, Projective
 verse
Voznesensky, Andrei, 104

Waley, Arthur, 46
Weightman, John, 107
West, Alick, 31, 32, 33, 42
 Crisis and Criticism, 30
Whitman, Walt, 50, 87
Wilbur, Richard, 57
Williams, W. C., 37, 38, 58
Winters, Yvor, 60, 103, 107
 Primitivism and Decadence, 102
'Woodbine Willie' (G. A. Studdert
 Kennedy), 28, 30, 36, 40, 41, 42, 43
Wordsworth, William, 46, 90, 112,
 129
 Prelude, The, 34
 'Vaudracour and Julia', 111–12

Yeats, W. B., 90–91, 96, 97, 117
Yevtushenko, Yevgeny, 104

Acknowledgments and thanks are due to the editors of the following in which some of the lectures have been printed: *The Sewanee Review*, *Shenandoah*, *Wascana Review*, and (particularly) *The Times Literary Supplement*.